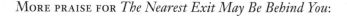
P9-CSA-896

MORE PRAISE FOR *The Nearest Exit May Be Behind You*:

"Life having the unpredictable crossroads it does, I've often wondered how memoirists handle the problem of writing a second book. Thanks to Bear Bergman's *The Nearest Exit May Be Behind You*, I know the answer: one goes about it with good-humored smarts, candid humility, and a queer and delightful generosity of spirit."
—Hanne Blank, author of *Virgin: The Untouched History*

"If we could just clone Bergman's brain and manners, the world would be a much better place, indeed. This new collection of meditations, essays, and stories about living visibly queer is complex in beautifully simple ways."
—Helen Boyd, author of *My Husband Betty*

"Bear Bergman writes circles around most people—circles that enclose so many identities, and so much insight about all of them, that you're bound to see some of your own selves newly, and beautifully, reflected there."
—Carol Queen, author of *Real Live Nude Girl*

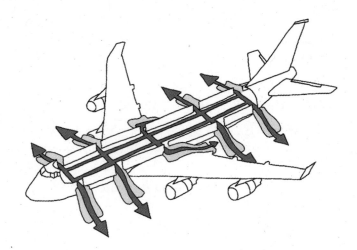

THE NEAREST EXIT MAY BE BEHIND YOU

S. Bear Bergman

To Brian —
Enjoy the journey — and all of them.
all the best —
S Bear Bergman

Arsenal Pulp Press
Vancouver

remember — you promised!

THE NEAREST EXIT MAY BE BEHIND YOU
Copyright © 2009 by S. Bear Bergman

All rights reserved. No part of this book may be reproduced or used in any form by any means—graphic, electronic, or mechanical—without the prior written permission of the publisher, except by a reviewer, who may use brief excerpts in a review, or in the case of photocopying in Canada, a license from Access Copyright.

ARSENAL PULP PRESS
Suite 200, 341 Water Street
Vancouver, BC
Canada V6B 1B8
arsenalpulp.com

The publisher gratefully acknowledges the support of the Canada Council for the Arts and the British Columbia Arts Council for its publishing program, the Government of Canada through the Book Publishing Industry Development Program, and the Government of British Columbia through the Book Publishing Tax Credit Program for its publishing activities.

"Not Getting Killed, With Kindness" was previously published in *First Person Queer* (Arsenal Pulp Press, 2007).

"Just a Phase" was previously published in *I Like It Like That* (Arsenal Pulp Press, 2009).

Cover illustrations by Karen Garry
Book design by Shyla Seller
Editing by Susan Safyan
Photograph of the author by Bill Putztai, *radiantpage.com*

Printed and bound in Canada

Library and Archives Canada Cataloguing in Publication

Bergman, S. Bear, 1974-
          The nearest exit may be behind you / by S. Bear Bergman.

ISBN 978-1-55152-264-7

          1. Gender identity. 2. Gays. 3. Lesbians. I. Title.

HQ77.9.B47 2009   305.3   C2009-903730-0

For my husband, Ishai
(there's a lot more to say, so if you don't mind,
I'll just take forever).

Contents

Acknowledgments

I'm grateful to a large number of people for their help in getting this second book (it's true! second books, much harder) out the door, and when I say help I mean listening to a lot of complaining, reading drafts, talking over ideas, telling me stories, taking my phone calls, consenting to appear in the pages under their actual names (and thus be indelibly associated with me), assigning my work to their students, and otherwise bearing my assorted nonsense with good grace. Especially, I love and thank Calvin Anderson, Toni Amato, Dr John Austin, Joseph Berman, the incomparable Miss Hanne Blank, Kate Bornstein, SJ Cohen, Ivan Coyote, Malcolm Gin, Sasha Goldberg, Rabbi Jon Haddon, Levi Halberstadt, Kate Larkin, Dr Robert Lawrence, the good boy Zev Lowe, Spike Madigan attorney-at-law, my brother dog Bobby Peck, Tori Paulman, Dr Carol Queen, my partner-in-crime Scott Turner Schofield, Gunner Scott, and (with extra laurels heaped upon his precious head) my husband j wallace, who inspired a great deal of this, and whose ideas and conversation fed both me and the narrative when we were failing. I am also grateful to each of the blog readers who took time to comment thoughtfully on drafts of new work, especially Dr Leigh Ann Craig, Laura Waters Jackson, Kerrick Lucker, Vinny Prell, and Rabbi Danya Ruttenberg. The households of 480 Chetwood, HALFLAB, and the House of Consent offered hospitality and inspiration of all sorts right along. Levi Jane lay on my feet very sweetly, and was usually quite patient about waiting for her walk. My family of origin continued to come through for me over and over again, most especially my patient parents, Carlyn and Michael Bergman, my spectacular brother and sister-in-law Jeffrey and Lisa Bergman, and my uncles David Bergman and John Lessner. All the fantastic people at Arsenal Pulp Press were, well, fantastic, and deserve great thanks, as does everyone who has ever invited me to come and give a talk, perform a show, or tell some stories for the folks where they are. For better or for worse, this book is at least partly your fault.

The Nearest Exit May Be Behind You

There I am in my seat, on a small commuter plane from mumble-somewhere to home—at this point, the travel details are lost to memory. What's still clear is that it was the last leg of a flight after several days of touring, that I was tired and somewhat wrung out from several universities-worth of hard questions and long performance days and explaining myself and my life and my loves over and over again, and that all I wanted was a little room, and a little quiet. I had aspirations of napping, or failing that, maybe some quiet time to respond to my always-on-the-verge-of-explosion inbox.

Neither one is possible, at my size and shape, with a seatmate on a Dash 8, which is one of those propeller planes with two-by-two seating up both sides of the aisle. I was seated toward the back, having chosen as usual to sit in row eighteen, seat C. Eighteen is a lucky number in Hebrew; since Hebrew numbers are also letters, the number eighteen spells out the word *chai*, or life, and I am a somewhat nervous flyer. The Dash 8 has twenty-three rows, so I was most of the way back, in my seat, and hoping to be left alone.

I had performed all of my usual magic to keep the seat next to me free. I hadn't buckled my seatbelt or moved any spare items into the free seat. I hoped, as I always do, that if I behaved as though I might gain a seatmate at any moment the sprites of air travel would be kind to me, and allow me to travel the last hour and a half from Wherever to home in relative peace and comfort. It often works. I was full of optimism.

And then I saw her. Coming up the aisle in a pastel twin set, those sweatery markers of women of a certain class, and some sort of frosted-bangs situation on her head, with a gold cross catching the dull airline fluorescent light. With the instinct born of long experience, I somehow knew that she was holding a ticket for Eighteen A. I watched her make her slow progress up the aisle, holding her bulging tote bag and wearing an expression of general superiority, scanning ahead to see who her seatmate might be.

Her eye fell on me. Her lips tightened, her eyes narrowed, and I thought I was seeing the single woman's customary response to the information that she was sitting next to big dude. I confess that I sometimes like to see this, actually—I have very good non-encroachment skills for such situations, and I was imagining quietly to myself how relieved she would be to discover that I could and would fly the entire way with my arms folded (to reduce shoulder span) and my hips shifted away so I could lean slightly into the aisle. I wasn't all that pleased to be gaining a seatmate, but I figured at least she and I could coexist quietly in the small space, and maybe the next time she was consigned to the seat next to a Big Fella she wouldn't make such a terrible face. What can I say? I'm an optimist.

I made as if to get up, so she could settle in without having to climb over me (just one more service we provide here at House of Fatboy), when I realized she wasn't slowing down at all. She was continuing past me, into the galley, to where the second flight attendant was waiting for us to sit the hell down so she could get back up front and do her preflight things. I assumed that she was going to take the long view of the cabin, to see if there was a free seat someplace that she could swap to where she wouldn't have to sit next to anyone or, failing that, perhaps someone with less specific mass. I wasn't offended—hey, I've done it too—and, in fact, I was a little grateful to think I might get a reprieve after all.

But when she got to the back, she addressed the flight attendant instead. "I can't sit there," she announced. "What other seat may I use?"

I barely had time to admire her correct use of the word *may* when the flight attendant asked the next reasonable question: "What's the matter with that seat?"

"I can't sit *there*," she repeated. "Anywhere else is fine."

"Ma'am, I can't help you unless you can tell me what the problem is," the flight attendant responded with a hint of impatience.

"I won't sit there. I don't want to put myself at risk of . . . catching anything."

The flight attendant looked puzzled. "Catching anything?"

My frosted erstwhile seatmate hissed, "The Gay. I don't want to catch . . . it."

My eyebrows flew up into my hairline, and I turned around. There was Miss Sweater Set, back to me, shoulders tense and arms akimbo, and the flight attendant wearing an expression I'm guessing matched mine. We were both dumbfounded.

Now, airlines have policies about such things. They will not reseat you because you don't like the look of your seatmate (perhaps I should say, they historically will not, though now that Flying While Muslim or Merely Appearing to Be Muslim or Perhaps Just Bearded has become such an issue, sometimes they flout this rule). But there are rules to prevent this kind of general-duty bigotry from being acted out, and both the flight attendant and I knew it.

She looked over Miss Sweater Set's shoulder at me, and sort of waved her hands questioningly. I could tell that she was leaving the choice up to me, either for reasons of personal values or to protect herself from a violation of airline policy, I couldn't say. Regardless, she was clearly bouncing this particular homophobic ball into my court.

I considered my options. On the one hand, I had the choice to more or less trap Miss Sweater Set between me and the wall of the airplane for the better part of ninety minutes, all told. I could read gay books, write gay smut on my laptop, discourse helpfully about the life of the modern homosexual. I could give a little *ex tempore* speech about Gays Throughout History, perhaps focusing on characters she would recognize. A little speculation, maybe, about the preferences of Eleanor Roosevelt, or the water-jug carrying man (a highly gender-non-normative behavior for a man of the time) who leads Jesus to the Last Supper as referenced in the Gospel of Mark, chapter 14. I could read to her from the collected speeches of Harvey Milk, or share some of the excellent research my wonderful friend Hanne Blank was doing for her upcoming book about the origins of heterosexuality. Or perhaps I could just take the opportunity to cough on her a great deal, complete with much apologetic touching.

Listen, I'm not a saint. It would have been a lot of fun.

But then I realized that if I relinquished this particular set of pleasures, I could have my seat to myself again; that the putatively sympathetic flight attendant was extremely unlikely to make someone else move to accommodate the homophobic wishes of what's-her-name. I could spread out my things, and my body. I could probably work *or* sleep.

In that moment, if I am being honest, I have to report that I had no compassion whatsoever for Miss Sweater Set. I like to imagine that I can act with generosity even toward people who avow themselves my enemies, and sometimes I really can, but in that tired moment I didn't care about her. I didn't even consider her. I thought only of myself, and how tired I was, and how much I was not equipped for any more toxic energy or misguided nonsense, and I waved her off. The flight attendant grumblingly reseated her (immediately in front of a screaming infant, I was pleased to note) and I buckled my seatbelt and raised my armrest and let my arms down.

Just after that, the usual safety demonstration was given. I generally tune these out, because I hear them twice a week on average, and they don't really change very much—one needs to be admonished only so many times to put on one's own oxygen mask before assisting one's companion before it sinks in. Likewise, I'm pretty sure that if you woke me from a drunken sleep at three a.m. and asked me where my nearest emergency exit was, I would mumble "it may be behind me," before glaring at you and going back to bed. I know all the words by rote. But somehow that day, after Miss Sweater Set's Catch-the-Gay hijinks, and my torrent of reaction to it, when the flight attendant said, "Please take a moment to locate your nearest emergency exit. Remember that the nearest exit may be behind you," I heard it in a whole new way, though it took a while for me to figure out exactly what had sent a shiver up my spine.

I considered it as I sat there. The flight was otherwise

uneventful. The flight attendant tried to apologize to me and I said firmly that it wasn't in any way her fault, and then I had a little nap. In comfort.

Of course, immediately after the plane landed, I called everyone I knew to tell them this story. They were all suitably, satisfyingly, both horrified and amused. People asked what I was wearing, what I was reading, if I had spoken to her or made some sort of eye contact, all of them dancing around the same question—how did she peg you as queer? Not only that, but what *kind* of queer did she think you were?

I have no idea, really. I wasn't wearing an expressly gay T-shirt, and my books and magazines were all still stowed. I don't know if she read me as a dyke or a fag or a tranny; have no idea what signifiers she was responding to (which, in retrospect, would have been the right reason to ask the flight attendant to seat her next to me). I don't know if it was my hair or glasses or clothes, comportment or demeanor, or just my general homotastic being. But something about me was clearly too queer for her comfort, and triggered a full-fledged Gay Panic that splattered all over me.

It's the nature of Gay Panic to do so. Even though the whole phenomenon is more or less entirely about the person experiencing it and their fears about homos (what if it talks to me? what if I like it? what if I, you know, *like* it?), it nonetheless is almost never contained where it belongs. Being visible in the world as a queer person comes with a whole set of these free-gift-with-purchase experiences, where you never quite know what you're going to get, or what it will end up doing. Indeed, this entire book consists of stories and essays written and told because the experience of being so identified on a plane made me start thinking in a whole new way about what it means to be visibly different, visibly queer in the old sense of the word, visibly and knowably Other.

Sometimes this is lovely. Sometimes it means recognizing your tribe, or knowing where to turn for shelter from a storm. But it also breeds a certain watchfulness. Once I finished chewing on the phrase, I recognized that I nearly always know where the nearest exit is, metaphorical or actual, when I am interacting with new people. I am nervous if I feel I don't.

So thank you, Miss Sweater Set, wherever you are. Thank you for sparking an entire volume of stories about how being readable as queer, as transgressive, as different, informs and shapes a life. However much you might not be delighted to have contributed to 200 pages of thought about queer and trans topics, I am nonetheless grateful, and hope the readers of this volume will be too.

While You Were Away

As a kid, I went to overnight camp for eight weeks at a time with a bunch of other Jewish kids from the Tri-state area who were also relatively happy, for one reason or another, to be separated from their parents for quite a long stretch. We spent our eight weeks doing arts and crafts, taking swimming lessons, evolving and disbanding highly complex preadolescent social structures, and trading the junk food our parents sent us for the junk food other people's parents sent them. There wasn't all that much to do, but there was a lake and long periods of indifferent adult supervision, so we managed just fine.

While we were safely away, making lopsided bowls in the ceramics shed, our parents tended to take advantage of our absences to do whatever needed to be done. More benignly, it was a kitchen renovation or a move across town. But for several years my bunkmates left for camp from one house, in one town, and were taken home to a different state. There were more than a few off-season divorces, a couple stints in rehab, and one of my more startled contemporaries returned home to discover that she was henceforth no longer living with her mom and dad, but instead with her mom and mom's new lesbian lover.

And now that you and I have had this little hiatus since you read my last book, it seems only fair that I should bring you up to speed on the changes in the last four and a half years since I finished *Butch Is a Noun*, got divorced from my wife Nicole, wrote and premiered *Monday Night in Westerbork*, lived alone for a couple of years, started this new book, fell in love at a conference in Milwaukee, moved to Canada, and got remarried—legally, this time, thank G-d for Canada—to a tender and brilliant activist and educator named j wallace (to whom I refer in this book by the fondest private name I have for him that's not too embarrassing: Ishai, his Hebrew name). Somewhere in those developments I seem to have gone from being someone people generally experienced as a dyke (or sometimes a straight guy) from an old suburban area of Massachusetts to being someone people generally experience as a fag (or sometimes a straight guy) from a big city in Canada.

Yeah, it's a little weird for me, too. For one thing, I use hair product now, at which suburban-dyke-me would have completely rolled my eyes, but somehow city-fag-me finds it essential.

When I write it out, it feels very far to have traveled. Much like it did when I was eleven and came home from camp to discover that the entire downstairs of my house looked completely different. My parents hastened to reassure me that it was mostly the same—even the same stove—but the paint, wallpaper, and carpet had all changed. Similarly, I have moved out of jeans and T-shirts and into capris and a summer fedora, but most of the underpinnings have stayed the same (and, in the end, it's still the same things that heat me up, too). I've let my little goatee grow in, started wearing earrings again, and painted my study a summery blue-green; it's all true, but this has not stopped me from also worrying all day about everyone and assuming everything is all my fault, though that last may be more about being a Jewish husband than being either a butch or a transguy. Sometimes these things are difficult to unpack.

I get a lot of questions, these days, about whether I'm still a butch or if I am now a transman. Truthfully, it's hard to say, a statement I make knowing full well that it just caused hundreds of readers to say, "Well, if you're not sure if you're a butch, you're *not*," and further hundreds to say the same thing, but substituting "transman" into the equation. I have to say, from where I'm standing, the lines are not nearly as clear as some people would prefer them to be, and the longer I hang around at various crossroads and deltas of gender, the more I notice that nothing is clear enough to be easy. Nothing about gender, or orientation, is clear enough to police or defend without circling the wagons so tight that we're all pissing in our own front yards within six months.

We all, perhaps especially those of us on the transmasculine spectrum, are sort of feeling our way along and sorting it out as we go. Me included. I talk a bit in this book about how hard it is to live so near to the site of so much battle, and how much I have been hurt by people's categorizing or dismissing or assuming about me. Mostly, what I have done is live into myself, into my faggot butch ways, from hair product to ass fucking, and frankly it's very nice here. And who knows what may yet come? If the last almost-five years have taught me anything, it's that I should be far more careful about the words *never* and *always*.

It's the sort of thing that happens, as we grow up and change. Maybe especially it's the sort of thing that happens to queers and transfolk because a lot of us spend our adolescences and early twenties—when straight, cisgender people are cutting loose and trying on identities left and right—figuring out how to survive and who in the world might possibly like us or love us or even just fuck us (and who we have to be to get that). The world opens, and we change a little more; someone from the other coast uses a new word that's like walking through a door into a whole different kind of possibility. Books are published, shows are mounted, art is displayed, poems are slammed, and stories are told, and each of these expands our understanding of identity a little more and better. Every one of them—every new story, every new word—creates a kind of opportunity to see ourselves anew.

The first one for me was the story of my great-grandmother, Bergie. She was named Rose Bergman, my father's father's mother, but she insisted everyone call her Bergie. I've always known about her, of course, but she died when I was small. Over time, though, facts have emerged. I know that she was the only one of my great-grandparents born in North America, the only daughter of the owner of a small hotel. She married in her late teens, had one son (my grandpa), and then abruptly divorced her husband and headed down to the Carolinas where she lived for years, leaving her son to be raised by her mother. No one knows what she did there, but when she came back she told her son that his father was dead, insisted everyone call her Bergie (not Mom, not Rose, and nothing else at all, ever) and never, as Grandpa told me, went near a man again. I also know that she was built broadly, with big hands—my dad tells me I have Bergie's wide-palmed hands—and used to row dory races and beat all the men in town in her funny wide little wooden boat. When I began to display my array of masculine behaviors in my teens, my grandparents told me a couple of stories about her. Before, I was awkward and odd and freakish in a bad way. But after? After, it was as though I was taking my place in something. Like I wasn't an ugly duckling at all, just a different kind of bird (though I don't think anyone would compare me to a swan, except for how noisy they are).

So welcome back. More adventures to relate, more thoughts to rattle hopelessly around in until I save myself or get spat back out, more stories to tell. Here's hoping you see yourself, in a good way, in some of them.

Wrap/t

The problem with the *tallis* I wanted was that it didn't match my dress. My dress, which had been chosen by my mother at Bloomingdale's from the Belle France collection, because Laura Ashley didn't make dresses in my size. My size, which by then was almost my current frame, including the collarbones my orthopedist once rapped his knuckles on and whistled over, the shoulders that forced the removal of shoulder pads from every women's garment I've ever owned. My shoulders, across which my *tallis* was supposed to rest gracefully, and somehow femininely, when I was called to the Torah for the first time, at thirteen, to take my place as a woman in the society of Jews, capable of adult authority and bound by adult responsibility.

But not, apparently, in matters of my own comportment. A campaign had been mounted to turn me from a bookish, sturdy girl into a Young Lady; it began with a new hairstyle complete with permanent wave, a hairstyle maintained with a round brush and a can of hairspray. With ears pierced long enough in advance so that I could wear "nice" earrings on the day of my bat mitzvah, delicate gold shapes that were a gift of my maiden Aunt Flora, the musician and scholar. And the dress, long shopped for and finally chosen, in blue and purple flowers, a delicate crocheted lace keyhole neckline, a slight bow at the back to nip in a waistline (or to create the illusion of one). The shoes, heels, black patent pumps so profoundly inappropriate for the occasion that I have no idea, to this day, what we could have been thinking; any homosexual in attendance surely spent my entire *haftorah* snickering under his breath. None of which I wanted.

I did not want the hair, the earrings, the dress, the shoes (or the imaginary gay ridicule, though that only in retrospect). I did want the *tallis*. I knew exactly which one—richly embroidered, with lions of Judea in relief on the decorative part of the shawl and a muted rainbow in the stripes. I couldn't describe it accurately in less than a page if you've never seen a *tallis;* if you have, you know exactly which one I mean. The point here is: that's the one I wanted. I understood, from previous conversations and the experience of my friends, that it was my choice—that, and the invitations. That was it, but still. My choice.

Instead, I got a cream and silver *tallis*, perfectly nice, the silver thread a little gaudy, but basically not bad. Neutral is how I have thought of it, and it is—neutral for a girl, especially a girl whose mother quite rightly discerns that she is unlikely to add a bit of glitz to an outfit on her own. My mother was looking ahead in her mind's eye to the photos, to me captured for posterity, photos that she would probably have to live with; maybe to future Rosh Hashanahs during which I would, of course, be glad. My mother, who has never owned or worn a *tallis* as far as I know. Twenty years later, the photos are in a lovely book that no one ever looks at, ever, and the photographic proofs are at home interleaved into my copy of *Bar Mitzvah Disco*, which I sometimes trot out for people who can't quite believe I ever wore blue eye shadow, or a blue-and-purple-flowered dress with a lace neckline, or gold seashell earrings that hung from rounded posts, or my parents' hopes about my femininity.

When I was first shown how to put on a *tallis*, it was by my old teacher Joe Yordan, a great teacher if perhaps a somewhat odd man. I have no idea how much his sense of mysticism influenced what he taught, but I remember him showing me how to pronounce the blessing, *Baruch Ata Adonai Elohaynu Melech haolam asher kiddishanu b'mitzvota v'tzivanu l'hitatayf b'tzitzit*, and then pull the piece of cloth over my head and let it rest there for a long moment—a breath, he demonstrated, two full theatrical beats—before settling it on my shoulders. I remember that we practiced and practiced, and that my movements were somehow not quite correct. My Hebrew was flawless—my Hebrew was always flawless—but it was a lot of weeks before he deemed my mechanics appropriate. He would show me again and again, and I would imitate him with all the skill a short but devoted life in theater had honed, but still it wasn't right. He would shake his head and sigh, and we would try again.

Again only in retrospect, it becomes clear to me that the *incorrectness* of my movements was gendered. Mr Yordan needed for me to perform a young woman's gestures, and now when I replay the moment in my mind's eye and think about the other bat mitzvah girls my age, they all did it the same way. Like grooming birds; a tender kiss each for the words *baruch* and *tzitzit*, a small motion of the arms, head ducking under the cloth and then up just in time for it to skim the tops of their heads. Elbows held close, chin slightly down, motions very restrained, they would wrap themselves in their *tallisim* in barely more space than they stood in (which, by the way, wasn't much. They *all* had Laura Ashley dresses).

And me? I was doing what my father did. He had, at the time, a long and slim *tallis*, a prayer shawl of somewhat retiring character, which he wore with great pride and a big man's motion. He pecked at the beginning and end of the blessing, quick and masculine, and then swirled it over his head in a movement that was in part commanding and also part kindergartener-learns-to-put-on-his-own-winter-jacket. He donned his *tallis* at full wingspan and with a kind of defiant pride, a post-World-War-II pride, a sense of himself as a Jew in a room of Jews. He would settle the *tallis* on his shoulders with a short tug, and when I was a kid I was amazed at the effect. My dad, my cranky overworked dad with his big head (a family trait) and mouthful of criticism suddenly looked . . . different. Calmer. When I was older, I would say that in his good suits (because, by then, he was wearing very good suits, tailored just right) and his *tallis* he looked like the king of a small but culturally rich nation. It remains true.

Nevertheless, my imitation of his *tallis*-donning behaviors was all wrong. I only know it now, because I can see it in hindsight and through the lens of what I now understand about Mr Yordan (and teachers in general, and also Jews, and also gender). I can see the disconnect, unbridgeable and unholy. At the time I was red-faced and frustrated, unable to understand what the problem could possibly be. In retrospect it's clear that this failure of behavior, of movement, was the same failure of my entire adolescence, wearing a different hat.

Truthfully, however, it must be said: if he had just told me to look more like a girl, I would have been able to save us both a lot of trouble. This was an instruction with which I was already familiar, and I had, by then, practiced with and gained a moderate amount of success at it (though, it also must be said, not so much success as all that). But either Mr Yordan didn't realize that's what he was asking or he somehow found the instruction odious; either way, he never asked that of me, just shook his head and showed me again, either unwilling to make the instruction explicit or unable to recognize the crux of the problem.

Regardless, I was always very attached to my *tallis* and, in the absence of specific instruction, probably went back to my tomboyish *tallis*-wrapping ways rather quickly, about which, after the bat mitzvah, I never heard another criticism. I don't think my parents wanted to fight that battle in addition to all the others—clothes, hair, school, and the rest of it, in the midst of which they may not have even noticed the *tallis*. I was not in company of great numbers among my contemporaries in continuing to attend *Shabbos* services and study after my bat mitzvah was over; I suspect that my parents were so pleased to see me close in the fold of Judaism that the angle of my elbow as I wrapped myself in my prayer shawl was beyond, or possibly beneath, notice.

If anyone else at *shul* noticed, they didn't say a word. Part of my experience as a gender-transgressive Jew was, and remains, in my family name and reputation. When we moved to Connecticut and joined our current temple, it was dying. I mean that literally; the elders of the *shul* were dying off or moving away, no young families were coming to take their place, and the building was crumbling around us. My family, along with a half-dozen others, worked tirelessly to turn the place around, holding fundraisers, firing the old rabbi (a mean man with no real *rachmones* and not much *sechel* either) and hiring a much better new one, scraping and painting and laying carpet and tile, teaching in the school. I worked alongside them starting when I was about eight years old and very earnest about it, setting up chairs and selling popcorn and scraping paint, and working in the kitchen with my father making platters every year to break our fast after Yom Kippur. So if anyone had anything to say about my problematically masculine *tallis*-wearing behaviors, they kept it to themselves.

Today, I accompany my family to *shul* for the High Holidays in a suit and tie, goatee trimmed and tidy, new *tallis* on my shoulders. My mother (Rabbi Search Committee, Building Committee, Board of Trustees) and my father (Ritual Committee, Building Capital Campaign, past Treasurer for seventeen years) introduce me (with an annually increasing note of insistence) as their daughter, Sharon, and it's not my first name that matters in that moment but my last name, my family name. It's the Bergman that trumps, that gives me the space to show up and be whatever gender of Jew I am. It's the family name that sees me through, again, and anyone who might still call into question the gendered behaviors of a fellow Jew in a Reform synagogue probably doesn't have the chutzpah to say it to me, a Bergman. So I sit with my family, in a whole row, with my folks and brother and grandmothers and cousins and, these days, my husband Ishai and sometimes even my ex-wife. I wear my *tallis* and hold hands with my relatives and kid around with my brother and cousins and help a grandmother up and down from her seat and, again, or maybe still, I am accepted for what I do, for having shown up at all.

Today, I Am a Man
(And Other Perorations of the Tranny Jewboy)

When the last (and best) of my great-uncles died, his youngest grandson, who was twelve at the time and almost six months to the day away from his bar mitzvah, cried inconsolably for three days. That's what my mother told me after speaking to his father; that he barely ate and hardly slept, alternated between refusing to leave his room and refusing to be separated even by one room from the rest of his family until the end of the first day of *shiva*, the Jewish week of mourning. All he did was cry, she told me, and no one could comfort him; he missed his grandfather so much already.

By the time I heard the story, over dinner with my parents a few weeks later, that cousin—the soccer star, the effortless charmer—was feeling better. On the third night of crying, he came down to the kitchen and helped himself to a huge plate of food, ate it all, killed some bad guys with his brother on one of their video-game systems, and then went to bed and slept twelve hours. After hearing the whole story, I commented, between bites of spinach salad: "Very Jewish."

My parents, who pretty much only get gender theory when I bring them some, looked puzzled. I swallowed and explained that I found it very Jewish to be hearing this story, told with great sympathy by my mother and his father, about a teenaged boy who cried for three days. About a teenaged boy who was *allowed* to cry, for three days, without reproach. Whose tears were explained with the sentence "Ezra and his grandfather were so close," and were only explained, not excused or erased.

I started to see understanding in my father's forehead, but my mother wasn't following yet, because she was never on the receiving end of the Boys Don't Cry experience. I admit that I forgot who I was talking to for a minute, and started sketching out a list of ways in which this was culturally anomalous within the standard North American, gendered culture. Teenaged boys are not allowed to show that kind of emotion, they're not rewarded for being demonstrably close with their families; usually they're derided as sissies or faggots for their "weakness" as evidenced through crying over a loss. Approval of men showing an emotion that isn't anger is a Jewish cultural value, I explained. So is the idea that being close to one's family is a quality of manhood.

(Please note that I am not suggesting that this or any other value is singular to Jews. When I talk about Jewish masculinity and enumerate its values, I am not suggesting that no other cultural group values these same things, nor that all Jews do so without exception. As ever, I am reporting and extrapolating from my experience of Jewish life.)

But let us acknowledge: in the vast landscape of American masculinity, from the Marlboro Man to Barry Bonds, Jewish men are not all visible in the same ways. We have the stereotype of the brainy Jewboy, the physician or accountant, who spent some portion of his boyhood learning to use his textbooks to ward off kicks. And while certainly there are exceptions, I am not the first to note that Jewish men, culturally long shut out from the kind of expressions of masculinity that define a more mainstream North American manliness, have created our own standards that depend more on academic achievement than athletic success, that favor being well-attired over being commercially attractive. Jewish men do not typically hunt, fish, shoot, drink, or fix cars; nor do they use force or even the threat of force to exert (or imply) dominance to get their way. However much this may be about class, it is also about the legacy of culture: Jews have historically not been permitted to compete openly with the culture of the ruling class in its own areas of achievement. In the thousands of years during which this has been true, we have adapted and come to value other qualities: intellect, skill at argument or debate, being bound to the family, storytelling (and, especially, good comic timing), and a certain sartorial flair, among others.

There are exceptions, of course. My father played football and lacrosse in college and used to drive an eighteen-wheeler; we have a family friend who is a total car gearhead and carries (and knows how to use!) a handgun. But my father's also the one who taught me the make-a-bunny-puppet-out-of-your-napkin trick for amusing small babies, and the guy with the handgun adores his family with an exuberance that is wonderful to watch and is also not, let us just say, prone to exerting much dominance over his wife.

But these exceptions lead us inexorably back to the rules. And in the rules, the advantages of Jewish heritage to the gender-nonconforming become clear. In the process of becoming a man, whether from boyhood or from some other gendered location, we model ourselves on the men around us. When we have good role models, we ape them, and when we don't, we take on the masculine characteristics we see modeled around us. Some of them are based on the actual behaviors of real men, and some on the cultural ideals of manhood we see or remember from childhood.

My young cousin, on the brink of manhood, will always be influenced by his grandfather's tender and engaged love of him, and he will also be shaped by the events surrounding his grandfather's death: that for three days, his father, uncles, and cousins gave him space to grieve, and that no one ever suggested, even once, that his emotional reaction was incompatible with his movement into manhood. That his brother and boy cousin, as well as his sister (all still children), also witnessed this will also bear out. When they are grown and faced with loss, none of them will think that their tears of grief, or the process of healing from them, are the exclusive province of femininity.

There is, always, the myth of the Jewish husband, much lampooned by comedians, a stereotypical man who might go off to work and be very much in charge, but who, upon his return home, is entirely under his wife's thumb (see, there's that story-telling thing again). The borscht-belt comedian Jackie Mason's well-known "comparison" between the Italian husband and the Jewish husband is not precisely a nuanced model of cultural sensitivity, but he does represent the stereotype well. Mimicking the Jewish man's workday full of people murmuring, "Yes, sir, yes, sir, anything you say, Mister Rosenfarb, Mister Goldenberg, yes, sir," he then contrasts this with the cry of this fictitious businessman's wife as he walks in the door at home, "You schmuck! You forgot to take out the garbage!" It's a known location, for me. I certainly know—hell, I have *been*—the model of the Jewish husband entirely in the thrall of his wife, taking a secret pleasure of ownership in accepting responsibility for all things up to and including bad weather, catering to her whims, and generally allowing myself to be always at fault. (My father's joke on the subject, usually announced in exclusively Jewish company, is: "Lincoln freed everyone but the Jewish husbands.") Living with that relationship model allowed me to move into a location of Jewish masculinity that I knew, and even if I did not always enjoy the individual moments of it, it felt familiar and, probably more importantly, I felt masculine. Manly, by a certain standard, and it was rather wonderful.

More than a hundred years ago, James Freeman Clarke, a Unitarian minister, abolitionist, and essayist, wrote an essay titled "True and False Manliness." A beautiful and profoundly feminist document, it says in part: "All boys wish to be manly; but they often try to become so by copying the vices of men rather than their virtues." When people ask me at lectures how my Judaism has affected my gender, I have the sense that they're usually hoping for some insight into Jewish law and ritual, gendered spaces, and the ways in which my particular Jewish community has, or has not, supported me in my gendered movements. But really, my gender was affected by my Judaism long before that, in the particular ways that being a Jew raised in an East Coast, Ashkenazi Jewish family with a fresh memory of the Holocaust pulled at me, at my gender.

As a girl child, I was never asked to be seen and not heard. I was chastised for being mouthy or a smartass, but never with any real force since family meals always included, or perhaps required, a lot of people talking loudly and all at once. Poppy, my mother's father, used to predict that I would grow up to be a lawyer every time I tried to get out of trouble by way of a technicality, but I knew that my commensurate punishment was always lighter if I either made my case, or made my inquisitor laugh (I assure you that no one to whom I am related, however distantly, is a bit surprised that I ended up being a writer and storyteller). This is not to say that I got an idyllic pass from all insisted-upon femininity—I did not, as anyone who has ever seen my bat mitzvah photos will tell you. In fact, I got a big dose. But Jewish girls, even Nice Jewish Girls, could be pretty *and* smart, at least in my Reform Jewish upbringing, at least in my family. I could have been a lawyer, doctor, or a nuclear physicist even, if I had liked math at all, or even been able to manage it. (And before you try to tell me that the math business is about inequities in teaching styles, let me assure you that all manner of people tried to teach me math, and to this day, the best I can do is calculate a tip quickly and accurately. In my case, this is not a limitation of gender.)

I honed my argumentation skills early and often, growing up in a family and a community that held friendly, even warm conversations at a decibel level that in other cultural contexts means the will is being rewritten as soon as the doors have been slammed. Any point could be debated, any story could be interrupted, and anyone might be able to jump in and either prove that they knew more about it or had a better idea. At age seven, my brother Jeffrey entered a family argument about nocturnal creatures (sparked, if memory serves, by some raccoon hijinks) and flatly contradicted my father's assertions about bat behavior by announcing that whatever-my-father-had-said couldn't be true because bats found their way around primarily through echolocation. My relatives shouted (yes, always with the shouting) with pleasure that he knew a good fact and a big word and had furthermore been able to make himself heard in the din, and he was promptly hugged and tousled while predictions of his future career as a doctor were made. It was some kind of surprise to me to learn as I got older that some people did not consider any part of this either normal or good behavior.

It is worth noting, I think, that in those childhood moments when my brother and I spoke up similarly and were wrong, we were shouted *down*, but hardly ever shouted *at*. It wasn't necessarily a sin to be wrong; you'd be corrected but not chastised for being mistaken. Later, in high school and university, I discovered how much this confidence and the relative fearlessness it created served me. A wrong answer? In front of everyone? Feh, I could do that five times before dessert.

This, then, was the location of dominance and jousting for position—in the war of golden brains and silver tongues. While some of the men of my family probably could have knocked someone down if they'd had to, in general, these debates reflect the Jewish value of argument and intellectual superiority as the way to master others and grow into adulthood. Where other cultural groups might be playing football in the yard or sparring in the basement or honing their marksmanship on the cranberry-sauce cans, the Jewboys are inside arguing about bats, practicing our own eventual ways of exerting our power in the public sphere.

The private sphere, a different matter. Jokes about overbearing Jewish wives aside, there is some strong legal language in Judaism that installs men firmly above women in public, legal, religious, and social hierarchies, and further: in an unfortunate but common response to the difficulties of being a lower-status person in the public sphere, some Jewish men exercise dominance over their wives and children because they feel emasculated in their business or public lives. I wish I could say that this has disappeared as the stigma of being Jewish has begun to ease, but I am not sure either of those things is true in enough places to assert it. When I was a Jewish girl I was keenly aware of the way I was encouraged to be smart and to learn to argue someone else into submission, but in my conversations with other young Jewish women of my class and denominational background, I've discovered that some of them were quite policed, though not as severely as is enculturated, with regard to their gendered behaviors in argument and debate. Still and all, as a Jewish value (if not visible in every family), women's learning and powers of argument cannot be denied.

As a woman, I was the third generation on both sides of my family to graduate from college, (and the fourth in the lines of two out of four great-grandmothers). We were born into a culture where girls and women have been taught to read and write for as long as we have history to tell. As a person learning to emulate manhood, the virtues available to me to copy seemed much more compelling than the vices, and also, in some cases, similar to the virtues held up to me as a Jewish girl, like academic success and financial stability. When I am asked, as I sometimes am, why transgendered Jews—and especially transmasculinely gendered Jews—appear, anecdotally, to be more likely to remain religiously affiliated, I say that this is part of the answer: It seems to me that we do not have to go as far, nor do we have to climb into places that seem quite as foreign to us. We can still cry and read and be sweet on babies; we do not have to learn how to spit or like beer (which is a good thing, as my fondness for babies is roughly as strong and unlikely to shift with gender presentation as my general distaste for beer).

In addition to emotional connectedness and intellectual success (with a heaping side order of argumentation skills), Jewish masculinity also tends to prize storytelling. I began this essay by telling the story that was told to me by my mother, as she heard it from my young cousin's father. As a people of diaspora, a people with a staggeringly long oral tradition, even considering our equally staggering literacy rate, there seems to be some . . . genetic selection at work. I have known good storytellers of many cultural or ethnic backgrounds, for certain, and I have known some Jews who could not find the beginning, middle, *or* end of a story with both hands and a flashlight, but I will say plainly that sitting down to dinner with a tableful of Jews guarantees good storytelling.

As an adult who is a professional performer, I am often asked about my training, as in: "With whom did you study storytelling?" Evidently, there are schools, and it is assumed that I am a graduate of someone's program. I always say with some seriousness that I studied storytelling with Arnie Friedlander. This reply has been published a few times, much to the delight of Arnie Friedlander, who is one of the best storytellers I have ever known in my life and is, by trade, in the building supplies business. Though I have taken a few storytelling workshops, I have not yet logged anything close to the hours I've spent listening to my dad and Arnie tell jokes and stories, entertaining a room. My brother and I (and a number of the other kids our age) have developed great comic timing thanks to them and all of the other less polished but still hilarious storytelling men of our family. This is something I have come to associate indelibly with masculinity; a man sitting back in his chair at the dinner table with a glass of something in his hand, smiling slyly, and saying, "I got one for you," in just exactly the right way. This is followed always by a short pause (which I now can measure out at roughly three beats, but I had to count my natural pause to know this) so that the laughter from the previous story can settle, and then, into the new quiet, a conspiratorial: "So." And the room is hooked again, knowing there's another belly laugh around the corner.

I can do these things. I can argue, explain, tell a good story, and love my family. I do it that night at dinner, the night my mother tells me the story about Ezra. I make my case and explain what I mean while my father questions me insistently about gender roles and what exactly that *means*, and how can you measure it, until dessert comes. I am halfway through the third illustrative funny story of the evening, which is actually about my recently deceased grandfather and his particular habit of doing all the dinner dishes before anyone else had gotten up from the table yet. I'm telling the story to make the argument about the complicated concept, and in the same moment that my parents get the gist of what I'm saying we all start to miss my grandpa, and we all tear up. I sniffle, my mother smiles the peculiarly lovely smile she gets when she's trying not to cry, and Dad looks down and away, tears flowing freely down his cheeks. I think, but do not say: Very Jewish.

Roadside Assistance

On my way from speaking to a conference of amazing students in Marinette, Wisconsin, to Milwaukee for the next set of gigs, traveling down Highway 43, I saw a truck pulled over to the side of the road, hood open, two sun-and-wind-reddened white people standing beside it, looking deeply unhappy. I pulled over, just behind, and asked if they were all right, if help was coming. The man, tall and beer-gutted and gruff, replied, "Do you know what's around here? We're dead in the water. I can't fucking believe this," before pacing a few steps away to squint at the nearest exit sign and then come back to the car window and stick his whole torso in again.

It didn't seem like the right time to mention that Mercury was in retrograde.

His wife was dancing in little anxious circles around him, trying to help but mostly just saying "calm down." I supposed he might be Asshole McStraightGuy, but I recognized the anger that comes from helplessness and frustration. I'm not, shall we say, immune to that either, and I was prepared to give him the benefit of the doubt even while he paced and swore. I pulled out my new GPS system, which has an I Need Help feature, and called up nearby service stations. When I found a promising one, I held it out to him. "There's a phone number," I said. He glanced at it and said, "I can't fucking read that. Can you read that?" he asked his wife, walking away from me again and puffing out air in upset little clouds. I offered to read it out to him, and he called a couple service stations, both closed. I offered to give him, or them, a lift into the next town to try to get sorted out, but then he walked away again to root through the truck without answering me—maybe to get a map, or his keys?—so I just kept calling garages until I got someone, and then passed him the phone so he could talk to the guy bringing the tow truck. While he used my BlackBerry, his wife explained that they were on their way back from their cabin on the lakes to the wedding of his favorite niece, which they were now definitely going to miss, a piece of information which made me even gladder I had passed his replies through my New York filter and not just gone off and left them.

When the tow truck was arranged, he came to my car and handed me back the phone, then stuck a big, meaty paw through the window and shook my hand, saying, in a much calmer voice, "Thanks. Thanks a lot." I just nodded at him and said, "Good luck. Hope you make the wedding."

I pulled away, lip reading through the window as he said to his wife, "Nice guy," and she responded with a sentence that started with, "He was, he was very nice, and you should . . ." I lost the rest when she turned around.

I wanted to say something else, though—almost did and then changed my mind in the split second before I spoke it. I wanted to say, "I need to say this: I'm a queer. I want you to know because, out of all the cars that passed you, I'm the one who stopped. I'm the one who stayed until your problem was solved." I am not sure if it would have even registered, if it would have been a safe thing to say while I held his hand, but in the moment of being there and play-acting this rough kind of helpfulness, I wanted to say it anyway. If he liked queers, if maybe he had a sister or a best friend who was of the lavender persuasion, I wanted him to feel well cared for by the great global homo conspiracy . . . and if he didn't?

Well, if he didn't, I wanted him to think twice, I suppose. I wanted him to feel humbled, or perhaps shamed, that his rhetoric or thoughtlessness might have harmed someone who went out of hir way to help him. I wanted him to look at LGBTQ people with new eyes. I wouldn't have minded some stirring music to go with it, either, and maybe a little speech about how I had changed his mind about faggots forever while his wife looked at both of us adoringly. Still holding hands, of course.

But here's the thing—the entire business got me thinking even more about why it is that I am always stopping on roadsides. Partly, I think, it's how much I like to be helpful (which, as my friends will tell you, is a powerful drive for me). But also, I think, as queers (and Jews too), we know what happens when everyone assumes that someone else will step up. In a rather intimate way, in all sorts of situations, we've been on the shit end of the I'm Sure Someone Will Do Something phenomenon too often to imagine that we're not also Someone. That we can help, and that if there's a risk to helping, the person may be worth the risk. And that, frankly, even if the person is not worth the risk, we remain the people who were willing to stop, to offer something.

I am not, by the way, limiting this to queers or Jews; I think that any group of people raised or grown into a mentality of the tribe, especially a tribe under siege, behaves in a similar fashion and understands what I mean here. In a situation of conserving resources, we learn to care first for our own. In networking, in making opportunities, we reach out to people like ourselves to give them a hand in some way. I have personally slept in the spare rooms of any number of strangers in any number of cities who were friends-of-friends or people I had spent a scant couple of hours with at a conference. When I teach my workshop, The LGBTQ Edge (about how queers and transpeople actually make better job candidates and should stop acting like it's a negative to overcome), I remind people of this. Always, someone puts up a hand and says that their experience of their racial or ethnic group works similarly. We know how hard it can be, and when we can, we will try to help.

I am also pretty sure this works in ways we don't consider. I learned a new one fifty miles later, when I saw a lopsided Buick on the soft shoulder with two small, white-haired persons peering down at the tire. With a sigh and a glance at my watch, I prepared to pull over again, only to veer off at the last minute when I saw a very large man dressed in full riding leathers, five days of beard growth on his face, and a bandanna tied on his head, halfway through changing their tire already. I pulled past the Buick and saw his custom Harley, painted with purple flames, parked just ahead of it. Maybe it's too much to assume, but I kind of imagine it must have been, at least in part, the same thing; a combination of innate helpfulness and a strong sense of responsibility, but also the prompting of being able to engage in a little good PR for Our Kind, whichever kind that may be.

It Only Takes a Minute, I

Every week is full of tiny gender moments, little queer vignettes, these rich and telling interactions that give me an endless running commentary about what the world sees in me (and how the world likes it). They're like story bouillon; please add your own voice and experience until they reach the desired strength and consistency.

In yet another airport van, I'm buckled in and waiting to go when we hold up for a late arrival. When he draws back the door, his eye falls on me first—maybe for having claimed the best seat, maybe for looking a little different. He takes a long look. I cock my head at him, then grin and say, "Sorry, buddy, you're not sitting on my lap." Everyone laughs, and he turns a little pink, then levers himself into the jump seat facing backwards, dragging his backpack awkwardly up behind him.

Fall fairs are my favorite. There are always a lot of small children to enjoy and a lot of fresh food to try. At the strawberry milk stand, I order a large and am told it's the last of it—news greeted with terrible howls by the children behind me (when I turn, they are cute and downcast). I ask the vendor to turn my large into two smalls, and attempt a quiet escape. When their mother says, "Tell the nice man thank you," and the older kid retorts, "Mo-ohm, that's a *lady*," I am already around the corner of the building and out of sight.

At our wedding, an old family friend—truly one of the nicest people I've ever known—marches around in great good humor introducing herself to people as having "known Sharon's parents for years." People look at her kindly, but as though she were a bit daft: that's very nice, ma'am, but why are you *here*? I finally find a minute to take her aside and remind her that no one else in the building except her and her husband, my parents, and grandmothers ever call me by that name; many of the guests have never even heard it. They all call me Bear. She nods and says she'll try it out.

Hardly anyone asks me, "Are you a boy or a girl?" anymore, not even small children. There were entire years when I'd get it at least once a week. I cannot tell whether this is because I look more firmly like one or the other these days, or because more people now know that this is actually a breathtakingly rude question. Maybe even packs of young boys, brimming with testosterone and bravado, just don't care now? Or maybe I don't trip their radar anymore. Can't decide.

Is it terrible if I say that I'm exhausted with talking about my gender? These days it's only so interesting, and only for so long, and the interesting part is over very, very fast. I still do it for money, because I'm good at it and because people still need to learn about it, but when I'm off work, I don't really want to explain things about gender any more than a dentist wants to peer into your mouth between the appetizer and dessert. Which is to say, not at all.

Dutiful Grandchild

The only thing of any real use I was ever able to do for my grandfather came just weeks before he died. He and my grandmother had, in consultation with my parents and uncles, decided to leave their home in Florida (where all New York Jews go to retire) and relocate closer to their children. They chose a senior citizens' residence building in Baltimore, a scant two miles from my uncles, and flew up to be in their new home while I drove their car north from Fort Lauderdale to join them.

I arrived on a sunny Wednesday morning, the day before their belongings did. A company whose sole task it is to move senior citizens had charge of their belongings, and it fell to me to meet them in Baltimore and get all of my grandparents' things settled, along with them, into their new home (and attempt to keep Grandpa from overworking himself and Grandma from driving everyone crazy by changing her mind every five minutes about such critical issues as which drawer the silverware would live in). After going in, greeting my grandparents, and giving a detailed recitation of my drive north, I prepared to go to the settlement office of the building to meet the people in charge of their new place, Susan and Becky. I shook out the wrinkles in my Hawaiian shirt, splashed some water on my face, and went down to the second floor to introduce myself, going over in my head one more time the introduction I had been rehearsing since somewhere in Macon, Georgia.

It had occurred to me sometime around then that my grandparents would have arrived three days before me, and would therefore have given Susan and Becky an endless round of details and impertinent information about me, their eldest grandchild and only . . . granddaughter. Sharon. I wanted all the moving and settling to go smoothly, without any unpleasantness about who I was or what I was doing there or whether I was my brother or what-have-you. Beyond that, I had no idea what Susan or Becky had been told about me, or who they would be expecting. Somehow I felt fairly sure, though, that it wasn't going to be someone like, well, someone like me.

But I was determined not to let a little thing like my gender get in the way of doing this service for my grandparents. And so I planned. I wore a shirt with great big flowers on it, gay as hell but perhaps readable as feminine if you, uh, squinted your eyes just right. I practiced pitching my voice up a little bit, too, just in case that might help. But mostly, I went over and over in my head some wording that I thought might make it clear to Susan and Becky, and whoever else showed up with the stuff, that I was definitely and legitimately the granddaughter they had been told to expect, regardless of off-season changes since my arrival in the world. I'd just finished a final rehearsal of the details when the elevator dinged. Second floor. Out I went.

I found my way down to the settlement office, confirmed the names on the door, and poked my head in, seeing two white women in their early forties both talking on two different phones. This was not in the plan. The plan had never been that they would get to have a good long time to have a look at me before I got started being charming and reassuring. I stood in the doorway, trying to look casual and yet still keen, while they finished their calls and took a leisurely look at my big ol' sweaty self in their doorframe, and I worked hard not to flee or simper. At last, mercifully, Becky finished her call and turned to me. Unfortunately, I was still looking at Susan, and so I didn't notice her finishing in time to start talking before she could say, "How can I help you, sir?"

Normally, I do not mind this. Normally, in fact, I like it fine. But today it was not helpful—today it meant I was starting from a place of having to work with a gender attribution already instead of being able to talk my way into some amusing middle spot. I took a deep breath, turned, and said, "Hi, I'm Bear Bergman, Rita and Stanley's—"

"Grandson! Of course. Welcome to Roland Park."

Shit. My mind started going a million miles an hour. Now what? Did I pretend to be my brother, hope no one noticed when my grandmother called out "Sharon" in ringing tones (and four syllables, a trick I have never been able to work out how she manages)? Did I 'fess up, make everyone feel uncomfortable, and hope Becky didn't decide I was too queer or too scary and take it out on my fantastic grandparents? I wasn't sure what to do, and frankly, though I'm often wrong, I'm much less often uncertain. I took a deep breath.

"Their granddaughter. Well, I started out that way, anyhow. They still call me Sharon," I said with a little laugh.

As soon as the words were out of my mouth I cursed them. What kind of a half-assed thing was that to say? Double shit. Bad enough I'm a queer and a shapeshifter and a gender outlaw, now I'm . . . wait, she's talking.

"Oh, I see. Great to meet you. Your grandparents are lovely people. Hang on—oh, Susan. This is Bear Bergman, the Bergmans' granddaughter."

Susan got up, greeted me warmly, shook my hand with both of hers. "You brought the car, yes? And you're here to get them all settled in? That's great. It's so nice to meet you; your father said you were coming down. Let me find out if the movers have arrived. Would you like a cup of coffee?"

I stood there for a minute, sort of dumbstruck. I think I managed to decline the cup of coffee, but I couldn't swear to it in court. I could swear that there was no sneering, no double-take, no homo weirdness, no tranny-what? Becky and Susan bustled around me for a few minutes and then took me upstairs where we met the movers.

My whole day went like this. I would show up, someone would smile and identify me as my grandparents' grandson. Then Becky or Susan or Grandma herself would correct them and say I was the granddaughter, and they would smile and say oh, wonderful, nice to meet you. Frankly, it was a little freaky. Granted that my grandparents were paying a decently hefty fee to live here, and also granted that my grandparents were, and Grandma still is, really extremely fabulous. But I could not figure out why no one was being even slightly weird to me, or questioning even the smallest bit why this big, tenor dude was the granddaughter. Maybe, I thought, they watch a lot of Oprah in Baltimore.

I stayed four more days, arranging furniture and washing plates and running to the store, taking photographs of things my grandmother insisted had been damaged by the movers and unwrapping the same tiny, sentimental items I marveled at in childhood but wasn't allowed to touch. I had the car washed and bought new hanging plants, coming and going from Roland Park multiple times a day. Whenever I saw Susan or Becky, or any of the other staff I'd met, they would greet me warmly and ask how Rita and Stanley were settling in. Just fine, I'd say. Doing fine.

It was almost the last day—Grandpa hadn't been feeling well at all, and was downstairs in the care wing—when I was sitting on a chair outside his room for a few minutes, that I realized why no one there gave even a very small crap about my gender or any presumptions it might have created about my sexuality. There was only one gender recognized by the staff there in people my age: Dutiful Grandchild. I could have been as outwardly peculiar as could be and it didn't matter, because I had shown up. That day, I realized that I was the only non-employee under fifty in the hallways. Sure, no one cared about my gender. In a building full of elders who had in so many cases been parked so they could wait to finish their days, anyone who showed up to help, to visit, to bring cheer or news or even lunch counted as a good thing. My gender was irrelevant, except as the Dutiful Grandchild. My internal narrative about being the Weird-Ass-Tranny-Butch-Grandthing-or-Whatever was entirely in my own head. In the eyes of Becky and Susan and the staff, I loved my grandparents and I had come to help. I could have been flossing the teeth of one head while singing Britney Spears tunes with the other for all they would have noticed or cared. Gender, schmender.

When I visit Grandma there now (my granddad died just two months after the move), she parades me through the halls like a trophy. I am her grandchild, come to pay her a visit. I visit as often as I can, staying with some of my favorite people in the world just down the road, and going to see my grandma twice a day. "All the way from *Canada*," she says loudly, "my granddaughter." Sometimes people say to her gently, as though she just can't remember the right words anymore, "You mean your grandson."

I always take care to correct them, cheerfully. "No, I'm the granddaughter. It's very nice to meet you, Mrs Birnbaum. Can I carry that for you?"

When Will You Be Having the Surgery?

It's true. I am trapped in the wrong body. And the truth is that if I could have surgery to fix it, I would in a hot second.

My problem is that none of the bodies into which I would like to live are available to me. Mine and everyone else's problem, maybe, I dunno, but my want of a different topography—however strong it may be and, oh, some days it sure is—isn't ever going to be but a patch on the problem.

If I could have surgery to be a slim, slight gentleman dandy of the 1920s, wearing high-button pants over no ass whatsoever and a fresh collar every Saturday night—that I would do. I would trade all this bulk and fur in a second to be the kind of boy that would have owned a selection of hatbands and changed them when he went courting according to season and occasion and whim. I imagine him pale as the beginning of time, blue veins ghosting through his skin and a dusting of blond hairs on his chest and legs, a slightly more robust swirl at his armpits and cock, but hardly enough to really sell Man. Tiny clothes, small enough to fit into the tiny suitcases of the era, the straw box with leather handle, out of which I could unfold a clean shirt every morning. Pull it on over my long limbs, snap my sleeve garters, cock my hat rakishly over my eye, give a grin, and take you out for a soda.

I would also cheerfully, delightedly have surgery to turn me into a zaftig redheaded girl, all tits and freckles, someone who could wear a corset and have it do for her what a corset is supposed to do: nip me in further at the waist and present my rack to the world on a velvet platter. The surgery would also have to give me her purring smoke-and-honey alto, her confidence with people of all genders, and her steady hand; the kind of girl who makes clerks and cops and passers-by fall in love for thirty seconds at a time all day long, who could linger over coffee or a short glass of good scotch all by herself and just watch the world go by, with not even a moment of thought that anyone would imagine she was by herself for lack of a willing companion. Always well-upholstered in pure cotton and silk, velvet and fine, fine wool, and I would slide her soft clothes on with no jewelry but my smile and think about what sort of company I wanted to call.

In fact, I would absolutely have the surgery to turn me into Mark-from-high-school, the blueprint of every boy I have ever been hot for since: short and stocky and fuzzy with a big ass and a ready smile and a kind, kind heart; Mark, who let me wear his denim jacket, which smelled like boy funk, for three days when I was a spectacularly awkward fourteen-year-old girl. I could certainly get my high school alumni office to tell me where he is now, what he's doing, but I don't even dare to Google his name, because, in my mind, he's well settled with a boyfriend who's sweet on him, and spends all his time designing beautiful houses that make people feel lucky as hell to live in. But to be him, yes, I would change everything in a heartbeat, wear only corduroy and shave twice a day, to live in his compact and handsome form.

It's true that I would probably have surgery to be more boys than girls, but frankly, I would also have it if I could have wings. Whenever I watch *X-Men: The Last Stand*, the X-Men movie with the heartbreaking winged boy, I catch my breath with a sob and no lie every time the tender teenaged protagonist spreads his wings for the first time. They look so beautiful, so absolutely right on him, pitching backward to steady him. They could lay me open at the spine and knit each nerve ending into me, make me wait longer and worse than any brand-new-girl with a new pussy ever had to wait with her dilating set, and I would still be cheerful. Even if I could never fly high at all, even if all I could ever get out of them was a little assist on a jump or a few powerful beats-worth of a soft landing, it would still be worth it. Totally worth it—and this is the place where, perhaps, I understand intense body dysphoria the most—to be able to look in the mirror and see them folded up behind me, to power or protect me.

I would probably have surgery for a tail, especially a prehensile one, but I wouldn't pay as much or endure as much: somehow, a tail seems more like an endlessly amusing sex toy than a thing one *needs*, and also I kind of have a hard time finding pants that fit me as it is. I might have chest surgery, but I don't usually want it because my big issue with my tits is how they *look*, and how they make my clothes fit—I really like the way they feel, is the thing, especially when my husband reaches for them. It turns out that through the magic of the Lycra undershirt (of which I now own several), I can eat my cake and have it too on that one. And now I'm a little bit through the looking glass there: ten years ago I was sure I would get a medically necessary double mastectomy in a heartbeat if I needed one, and now I feel less excited about that. I would definitely have surgery that would fix my weight permanently at about 245, which seems to be the right weight for my frame and leaves me big and bulky like I prefer, but not *quite* so doorway-filling as I am now and would be so much kinder to my knees I cannot even describe it. I seem to be permanently set on

275, though, in various configurations of muscle and fat, which is fine but not quite what I would prefer, so if I could set that dial I totally would.

I would have surgery to make my reaction to the bitter Canadian cold less severe, even though I now have two full sets of performance-weight under-layers (one wool, one polypro) to keep me warm, and I would have surgery to end, once and for all, my miserable cystic acne. I would have surgery to improve my knees, my balance, my eyesight (even though I might still choose to wear glasses, because I think they really suit me), my terrible temper, or my sense of direction. I might even, if it all worked the way I would want and I for *sure* wasn't gambling with my ability to come ever again, have surgery to have a penis attached (especially if I could have it attached, I don't know, maybe a little higher than usual so I could keep the other good stuff I like as well).

But if I can't go from the body I have to a body that I am certain would feel very right—right like having wings would be or even right like wearing spats would be—then I think, maybe not for me. Which isn't to say not for you, of course. You should move toward whatever changes, whatever surgeries, whatever renovations or alterations or restorations will create you in the glory you deserve, oh yes you should. And you should do it with your usual style, and you should do it without shame, and when you're healed up and ready we can go shopping for something fabulous to showcase the many wonders of you.

But me? I might actually be waiting less for advances in surgery and more for advances in time travel. We'll see. Meanwhile, there are a lot of reasons people don't have surgeries. Okay?

What's in a Name?

About once a week, I have the following exchange when I introduce myself:

"Hi, I'm Bear Bergman," I say, reaching out to shake hands.

The person to whom I am introducing myself, instead of volunteering hir own name (which is the traditional form), replies instead, "What's your real name?"

Granted, I live in the world with what some people would consider a somewhat unusual name. And when I say "some people," I mean mostly white, anglophone North Americans, usually those from the northeast and sometimes the Midwest of the United States. Southerners, upon introduction, often think I must be named Paul (after legendary football coach Paul "Bear" Bryant), and think nothing of calling me Bear, but do tend to follow up asking what position I played. On the West Coast, people named Zephyr or Trash or Puppy are so common as to be entirely unremarkable. People might guess that I was born in a commune or decide that I chose my own name, but either they don't care or they want to Honor My Process. Everywhere else in the world, well, it's not their language. They just smile nicely.

In some ways I am grateful for having had ten years of this experience already, even before I started to grow into my gender and look more like a man to the casual observer, more of the time. Because while naming is a fascinating thing worthy of much conversation, it also turns out that some people enjoy a particular parlor game of learning the birth names of transpeople.

There are many traditions, most of them religious or spiritual, that seem to have contributed some power to this current of interest in learning someone's birth name (which many believe to be the True Name). Some Pagan traditions believe that knowing the True Name is a powerful kind of knowledge about someone's character or nature, and that it is with the power of the True Name that someone can be located or called spiritually. Jews, especially Ashkenazi Jews from Eastern Europe, will never name a newborn after a living relative, because they believe that the Angel of Death is looking for elders whose times are up by name, and might take a baby by accident if the child had the same name as the adult. This belief among Jews is so strong that sometimes, if an infant or toddler becomes gravely ill, hir parents will change hir name in an attempt to confound the Angel of Death into going away empty-handed. Catholics give young adults the name of a saint upon the occasion of their confirmation, adding the holy name to their birth names to cement the relationship between that person and their patron saint (and, I was interested to learn, children of any gender can take on the name of any saint—the choice is about that saint's qualities, not hir gender). Many First Nations who have kept their naming traditions will give a child a temporary name at birth, a name that serves to welcome and honor them, and only at a further stage of development, when a young adult has become someone with personality traits and interests, does a group of people within the community (sometimes including the person to be named) choose a permanent name for that child. Among the Chinese, the modern custom is for people in business to have an English name, to the degree that human resources forms have a space for it. This both conveys the fact or appearance of having attended an anglophone university (considered a boon) and removes the difficulties of more traditional, relational forms of address used in social contexts, where you might be known as Third Son or Tall Wu. And so on—there is a reason that the study of names and naming crosses psychology, anthropology, sociology, and linguistics, and even has a subspecialty, phonosemantics, which suggests there may be an intrinsic relationship between sound (the spoken name of a thing) and the nature of the thing referred to. I mention all this because I want the weight of years and research and authority behind me when I say Names are a really, really big deal.

I introduce myself as Bear Bergman. I am greeted at the bank, pharmacy, and dry cleaners as Bear. I work as Bear, and my friends and lovers all call me Bear (unless they have a private, fond nickname for me), and I sign checks as Bear. The people who still call me by my original, given first name have known me since before I made my bat mitzvah. To these dozen or so mostly octogenarian people, I have given explicit license to go on calling me Sharon. I will also answer to Sharon for people who are employed by the air travel industry, for whom even Jay-Z must appear as Shawn Corey Carter, passport (and custom lavender Timberlands) in hand. Other than that, I am Bear, and I consider this to be my real name because it is how I think of myself, what I'm called, and what I answer to.

(Department of irony: in order to find out how Jay-Z was named on his birth certificate, I turned to Google. And what search string did I type? "Jay-Z real name.")

I was named Sharon after my great-grandfather Samuel, my mother's grandfather on her mother's side, deceased shortly before I was born. It's common enough among Jews to give a named-for child just the first letter of their antecedent's name, sometimes along with that person's Hebrew name, and I remain eternally grateful to my parents for not choosing to name me Samantha. As sometimes happens, though, my birth name stopped fitting me well around the time of my adolescence, and I was renamed Bear twice in pretty short order by two different groups of people who had no point of overlap. Not being an idiot, I took it on, and allowed the name Bear to become more and more present in my life. Earlier I was hesitant, in large part because of questions like, "What's your *real* name," but as I became the person of my name, I learned to defend it as I would anything else I liked.

People are often curious—sometimes unkindly so—that I don't insist that the last remaining holdouts (my parents, grandmothers, and a couple of old family friends) call me Bear instead of Sharon. For me, my change of name was not and continues not to be related to my change of gender. So my struggles with my relatives (and people I have known so long they might as well be) on the subject of my name is more in the realm of the practical: Please try not to use my first name when introducing me to new people, lest I have to make them *un*learn it. Please try to remember not to make out my birthday cards addressed to Ms Sharon Bergman, and especially not the birthday checks, because checks made out to that person will not be cashable at the bank by Dr S. Bear Bergman, which is how the nice people at my bank know me (having conferred the title Dr on myself to avoid gendered honorifics). Etcetera. It is also worth noting that one of the few things in my world about which I am secretive—except, I suppose, not anymore—is that I do not insist my parents use the name Bear. I especially hide this from parents of newly out transpeople I know. I do not want them getting the idea that there's a parallel to be drawn: if it's okay for my folks and with me, it must therefore be okay for them to continue using their child's birth name. It's not a parallel because I have never asked my parents to call me Bear, while many transpeople have asked or demanded or begged their parents to call them by their new names, but in the dim corners of denial many subtleties are lost. So I keep my mouth shut about it.

For some transpeople, the mere invocation of their former names is a source of stress and anxiety. It makes sense. For lots of transfolks, the very first thing they have the agency to change is their names, and hey—trannies are no less in the thrall of naming than anyone else. Many people's first step out of the Big Box o' Standard Gender is to rename themselves for their new journey, perhaps the most universal rite of passage across time and geography and culture. There's a reason for this: a new person demands a new name. We know this instinctively, perhaps genetically, even if we cannot point to or prove exactly why. Of course, a newly out transperson is not entirely a different creature, any more than someone in any of the above, culturally defined name-change scenarios is. But perhaps there is a line of newness beyond which a new name is demanded. Regardless, we as transpeople are fond of our new names, and sometimes afraid of our old ones.

I do not hate my first name, but I am aware of who uses it or even wants to know it, and why. Elder relatives and airport security people are, well, who and what they are, and their motives aren't problematic to me. But often new acquaintances will query me avidly and with an odd sense of entitlement—or, more regularly, demand to know—what the S. in my name stands for.

There's something about my choice to leave my initial out where anyone can see it but not use it that is apparently too tempting to resist. US lawyers refer to this as an *attractive nuisance*, like when you leave the pool in your yard unfenced. It's not that my first name is a secret—you've read it ten times already if you've got this far in the book—but I'm on my guard anyway. I know that some people like to make their own rulings about what's valid in the worlds of transpeople (a topic treated more thoroughly in the chapter called "The Velveteen Tranny") and that they will call me by my first name no matter what I say.

In training sessions for provincial Human Rights investigators about trans issues, one of the first kinds of trans-identity-related harassment I make certain to cite is the tactic of calling a person who has transitioned by hir former name repeatedly, with the intention of being disrespectful. Maybe it's this history that makes me wary, but when I introduce myself and people ask me what my real name is, or what the S. stands for (if they've seen my book covers or something), I pause. It seems like revealing an intimate fact to answer the question, and if I do not feel intimate with someone, then the question is jarring and intrusive.

(I have a fantasy list of intimate questions about names I consider asking people in return, focusing on who they were named for or why their names were chosen, or how they decided to change their names with marriage. Turnabout seems like fair play, and if I am expected to answer intimate questions about my name from relative strangers, then it seems only fair that I should get to ask them as well.)

This is often, but not always, a diversion of the cisgendered, sometimes accomplished by guessing, sometimes by demanding the birth name of someone too young or startled or disempowered to tell them where to stick it, sometimes by means of trickery or research. I do not generally consider it malicious, except in cases where someone then *calls* their target by that former name without permission, which is about as rude a thing as you can do to a transperson. In the Angie Zapata murder case, the defense attorneys called her by her former, male name over and over and over, trying to hammer home the idea that she had perpetrated terrible, tranny trickery on her murderer. It backfired. The use of her former name was correctly seen by the jury as disrespectful, and the combined disrespect of client and attorney bought Allen Andrade a sentence with a hate-crime addition, totaling life in prison without possibility of parole. The naming issues crop up instantly whenever the news involves a transperson.

This particular news will be outdated by the time this book is in your hands, but parallel things happen often enough. Aiden Quinn, a Boston transit driver, caused a crash while text-messaging with his girlfriend. He's a transguy, and so instantly all the news outlets started digging around in his records to see what they could find out, outed him as a transsexual, and some of the sleazier ones started referring to him as Georgia "Aiden" Quinn. It's become a shibboleth of trans-awareness in much the same way that in 1999, when *Boys Don't Cry* came out and the case was repopularized in the media, you could tell a lot about a newspaper by whether it referred to the murder victim as Brandon Teena (as he preferred) or Teena Brandon (the legal name of the deceased at time of death).

The flip-side variant among transfolks is to be shown the yearbook or former identification card of a transperson, with their old name and haircut—a kind of fond bonding ritual, a way of taking someone into confidence with information you fully trust that they will not use against you. This naming thing, it's tender stuff, like showing someone your alarm code. You have to trust that they won't sneak in and harm you, that they can carry sensitive information and only use it in a moment of genuine requirement. That they won't allow you to be called out of your name, even after your criminal conviction or untimely death.

Me, I do neither and both, as usual. I carry my first name around; I cannot quite allow it to pass into Former Name status, and yet neither can I really embrace it anymore. Sometimes, when required to use it for travel or banking purposes, I pronounce it in the Israeli fashion, Sha-RONE, like the former Prime Minister. It has the effect of masculinizing, of providing an alternate narrative for these commercial encounters that explains why the big dude in front of them has a girl's name. I once spent the most satisfying fifteen-minute hotel-check-in of my life bonding with a young guy named Mychell. His name, pronounced the same way as Michael, evidently often causes people to pronounce it as Michelle and/or expect to find a woman answering to it. In retrospect, I can only wish I had recorded his elaboration on his name. He shared his empathy at having a name many people read as a woman's name, honored his mother for choosing it, cited that as the reason he would not change it, and talked about the cultural arrogance of the United States and how we're so quick to believe that we understand the gender of names when we really don't, as he succinctly put it, know shit about it. I shared with him the tidbit, usually reserved for lectures, that about half of

Bengali men's names end in a vowel, which is a strong marker of a female name in North America. He shook his head and laughed. Then he wished me, under my masculinely pronounced female first name, a very good night.

New Year

This whole story would never have happened, except that the day after Christmas it began to rain. I try to remember that all of these lovely, funny moments are always out there just waiting for the right moment, or weather, but it's difficult to see except in retrospect. And then when you get them, you have to use them right. It's harder than I remember, every time, but the payoffs are good. I assume you all know this, but I am writing the story down here to help me remember.

This year, at New Year's Eve on the Gregorian calendar, Ishai was supposed to be off skiing from hut to hut in the backwoods of Quebec on a trip I had arranged for him as a Chanukah gift, and I was supposed to be having a visit from Zev. But it started to rain, and it kept right on raining, and by December thirtieth—when Ishai was supposed to leave—it had rained so very much that they closed every provincial park in Quebec to skiers. But Zev arrived on schedule and so, between one thing and another, we all three found ourselves looking for a place to have dinner the next night, on New Year's Eve, a holiday none of us celebrates (two Jews and a Muslim walk into a buffet . . .) but which tends to play merry hell with one's dinner options. We finally settled it that we'd go for dinner at the best of the local Indian buffet places, which had good food and was open and seemed like more than enough festivity for us. As we arrived and waited to be seated, my beloved husband and I smooched a little, feeling snuggly and fond. When we stopped, I saw a table of three to my left actively and animatedly (with gestures) debating our genders.

I loathe this. I don't know why it bothers me more than other gender-related unpleasant behaviors, but it does, it screams of rudeness. Sometimes I just smolder, sometimes I go over and make a snarky comment about gender nonconformity not being positively correlated with hearing loss, sometimes I ask from where I stand in ringing tones if they could be any more rude. I have been known to approach and simply stare, puffed up and looking as imposing as I can, until they turn away or mumble an apology. I get terrifically activated by it. What's worse, I cannot seem to stop, even though I try very hard to remember everything I know about gender and about kindness and about people and how we are all just trying to make it work as best we can. In a serious and worrisome way, however, this has not been a location of good behavior on my part. Nor has it been good for me.

Perhaps because I was in pleasant company, perhaps because it was right on the cusp of a new year, that night I took a deep breath, and somehow managed to make a different choice. I went to my seat quietly and thought about what to do, and I tried not to seethe or fume or snap at my dinner companions. When I got up to go to the buffet, I took the waiter aside and quietly told him I wanted to pay for their dinner, and to please add their check to mine. It somehow deflated me a little. I let out my long-held angry sigh and refocused on the food (tasty) and the company (ditto) and how good it smelled in the restaurant and how pleased I was to be wearing my nice new shirt. I had an idea of what might happen with the gender-performing strangers. But mostly I felt calmer, and was better company at dinner, and enjoyed my meal more. Most importantly, I wasn't angry with them anymore. Sometimes I really resent that whole thing about forgiveness and kindness and how it makes *you* feel so much better—I am pretty much a New Yorker, after all—but it totally works.

I intermittently kept an eye on their table. After a while, it was time for them to pay, and the pantomime I was able to read from across the room was pretty much what I had anticipated. The waiter explained that we were picking up their check. They looked puzzled, talked about it a bit amongst themselves, and elected their representative. The guy who had been dining with two women walked over looking cheerful but a bit hesitant. He said that they'd told him we were buying their dinner, and thanks very much, um . . .

I stood up and introduced myself, Ishai, and Zev before he had an opportunity to get any further. We shook hands all around. He went on to say thank you again, and that it was so nice, but . . . had we met before? Was he forgetting us? He fumbled his way through his questions, trying hard to figure out why we were buying their dinner without offending us in case we were old friends from university or business colleagues he didn't recognize out of context or, er, something.

Taking a deep breath, I simply said that we'd noticed them talking about us when we arrived, and that we'd thought they might like a reason to come over and meet us in person. And then I shut up and waited.

He paused, dropped his head a little bit, and took a breath. To his credit, he didn't dissemble or try to offer some sort of junk excuse. Then he said, sort of quietly, "That's a remarkable gesture," and picked his head back up and shook hands all 'round again. As he did, he said, "It's good to meet you," and he sounded as though he genuinely meant it. We wished each other a happy New Year, they left, and we had dessert.

I cannot tell you how satisfying it was. Partly because I was able to manage that kind of interaction without losing my temper for blessed once, and partly because they got the point in a far clearer and pointier way than any stare-down or snarky comment had ever got it across. Plus, to be honest, the look on his face when he realized how very busted they were was worth far more than the fifty dollars I paid for their dinner. But busted with kindness. That's the trick.

I wonder about how to apply the same lesson when I don't happen to have the spare cash to be buying dinners, or when the venue is different. Perhaps a little gender-explanatory card and a cupcake (which I would carry with me at all times)? I'm not sure. To be honest, I haven't figured it out all that well, and often my desire to protect and defend the people I'm with is much greater than my interest in remaining centered on kindness. It is, however, entirely true that I felt great about my New Year's escapade for weeks afterward. Even if it wasn't perfect, it was better than I had ever done before, and eventually I decided that "better than I'd ever done before" was more than enough to ring in a New Year.

The Velveteen Tranny

I. Theory

I think it would be a very nice thing, to be real.

I don't know for sure. I've never been real, and so it's a bit hard to say. Perhaps there are things about being real that I wouldn't enjoy. But considering the tone and flavor with which I am generally, and have across my lifetime been told I am not real, I assume it must be better. Or, at the very least, that there must be some benefit, if only because so many people *think* it's better than being. . . the things I've been. Not fake, quite. I'm rarely told I'm fake, but I can't imagine why since it seems clear that fake is the opposite of real. Doesn't it? Never having been real, again, I am not sure.

I wasn't ever a real girl, except, I think, when I was so young that I wasn't myself at all, just an extension of my parents' projections about me. I do have photos of myself in dresses with pinafores and petticoats, and I am certainly smiling pink, gummy smiles in them. But it's not long before, in the pictures, I am wearing blue jeans and T-shirts, or grubby shorts showing filthy knees from playing explorer games in the vacant lot with the kids on my street. I played basketball with Michael Carroll, who was fifteen when I was five and must have grown up to be a great dad, as patient as that boy was. My realness never took hold, as a girl, despite all the ways anyone ever tried to make me more real from the outside in, as though if enough eye makeup were applied it would eventually sink in through the skin. I tried and failed, and tried some more.

That narrative is only a little interesting at this point; only useful as a cautionary tale to parents who keep trying to paint some normative gender on their children in the hopes that it will make them more acceptable to the rest of the world. It won't. Please, stop trying. It doesn't make the rest of the world like us any better, because they can almost always still see that we are somehow, ineffably but unmistakably, not real, and now not only that but we can hardly recognize ourselves. It's better for everyone if you can start getting used to your gender-non-normative child now. If you can't manage to buy him a tutu or her a tool belt, that's okay for the moment, but please at least invest in lots of art supplies and science toys, and stop trying to hand your boy a truck when all he wants is a doll, or your girl a pair of dress-up angel wings when any idiot—and you're not an idiot, are you?—can see that she's long on grounding and low on gossamer. If, as children, we can't be real to the world, it's always way easier if we can at least be real to ourselves at home as much as possible.

Eventually, I was a butch. I was never a butch lesbian or a butch woman, though I probably was a butch dyke for a bit there, but only situationally. I always said that butch was a gender all its own—yes, a noun—and I was pretty clear that that was me. I was a masculine female, a he-she, an egg timer in a forest of hourglasses, and for a time I did okay as a butch. People believed in it to a degree and let me keep my noun on credit, but heads were shaken, and plenty of people told me I wasn't a real butch. Real butches always and only love femmes, and while I adore femmes and have loved several in my life as well as I could, I didn't love only femmes. I melted over other butches. I cruised burly, grey-haired butch daddies twice and three times my age, butches who had kids older than me. Butches who had boots older than me. And I had no skills in the trades, and I couldn't fix a car. One year, for my birthday, I received a dozen tire gauges from various people as gifts because I thought the channel sewn into my friend Kage's mechanic's shirt was for a pen, and everyone thought that was so funny they all got me tire gauges (which, it turned out, is what the spot is really for). I still have one of them in a drawer of keepsakes, but I've never learned how to use it, like all the real butches. I never wanted a motorcycle or a muscle car or a fishing pole or a motorboat; never worked construction or painted houses. I usually took care of kids or fiddled with computers for work, and the one appropriately butch job I had was working the door at a gay bar, a job I got because my conflict de-escalation skills were better, in ratio to my specific mass, than any of the other applicants.

But as a butch I was kind of . . . girly. I didn't like to camp or hunt, I didn't drink beer, and my pool game is a disaster. I liked to read and write and brunch and shop and cry and go to musicals. I was scared of horror movies, and my favorite part of the Super Bowl was always the commercials. My friends liked me anyhow, certainly, but they took these opportunities to tease me about what a real butch I was definitely *not* when they arose, as with the tire gauges. Or my haircut, which I wore in a flippety Prince Valiant style for some time (because it fell nicely into place without having to put product in it and, on a good day, made me look a little bit like Joey Lawrence). But my buzzed and butched and flat-topped friends gave me so much shit about it, asking when I was going to get a proper haircut for a real butch.

I tried, I swear I did. Not as hard as I did at being a girl, because I was more stubborn and less dependent on the approval of my criticizers for things like food and shelter, but still. The thing is, it wasn't really the activities or the hairstyles that got me in trouble, that prompted people to comment on how real I was not—those were just the signifiers, the concrete, recognizable things they could point to. But unlike my girlness, their unsettledness ran deeper. There was some discomfort with my performance failure but, I now believe, a much greater amount of discomfort with the fact that I didn't really seem to be working hard to do it right. I wanted to be real, but not fakely real, only really real—real in myself and also recognized as real.

It gets so complicated. Being real, being read as real, being real to myself. Are we all more or less performing something we hope reads as a workable gender, praying no one notices how we're really, seriously, irrevocably fucked up? Hiding carefully how far we have strayed in our hearts from the ideal that gets packaged and sold as realness? Thinking about how much we would cheerfully pay to get a few days off to go somewhere nobody knows us and indulge in all our unsanctioned realnesses without anyone there to drag us back to reality? I think we are.

And then I went and made it all worse. When I finally stepped back and looked at all the pieces, trying to figure out which gender really seemed like the best fit, the one most satisfyingly for *me*, I kept circling back to faggotry. Queer men can be fashionable and cry while simultaneously being burly and wearing suits. They probably—we probably?—have the greatest amount of freedom to shake up gender into something I find really fun, as long as we're prepared to pay for it with our lives, if necessary. No queer man has ever looked at me funny when I said I collected vintage cufflinks, which is pretty well at the intersection of all of the identities I have ever had (and has gotten me laughed out of more than one conversation). For a long time I said that I was definitely never going to transition to male, because I wouldn't be any better at being Man than I was at being Woman; that if I transitioned I would have to buy tutus, so I might as well save the money and be a gender outlaw in my original sex and butch gender. Certainly I was very practical. Certainly I understood where in the world I stood the best chance of eventually gaining realness, and so I publicly resolved—in writing, even—that I would remain firmly situated in the previously agreed-upon location of butch.

But I didn't quite stay there. Partly, I couldn't seem to make my point about butch as a gender, and people kept insisting I was a butch woman or, more problematically, a butch lesbian. More than one charming femme actually said to me, "I'm so glad you're staying a lesbian," and each time my heart sank; each time I felt like I had been erased. Also, as it turned out, I was rather more suited to the tutu style of gender variance than the carburetor style. I was more *Queer Eye for the Straight Guy* than *The L Word* by a factor of, uh, kind of a lot. And so, after some conversation internal and external, I shuffled just a tiny bit there over the line of masculinity into something closer akin to manhood, hoping for authenticity, hoping for my chance to become real. Hoping to finally find a quiet place of gender I could ease into.

Man, did I ever not find it (pun intended). I didn't know, before I made my little shuffly hopeful move, about the great and terrible truth of transgender life, which is that they will never let you be real, ever again. Not even if you absolutely promise and completely swear to follow every directive from the Home Office immediately upon receipt. I didn't know it when I signed on—maybe I should have, but I didn't—but the transperson is always a knock-off, as in, "Why would you date a fake man when you could have the Real Thing?" (strut, strut, posture, posture), and ze is always the location of deceit.

It must be true, or people wouldn't respond the way they do. Kate Bornstein famously asks, when people ask if she's had the Surgery, if they mean her nose job. She jokes about it because she has been talking about transfolks, and her own trans experience, in popular culture longer and better than anyone else, and after the millionth iteration of some stranger deciding it's okay to quiz you about your genitals after thirty seconds of acquaintance, let me tell you . . . if you don't make a joke you'll scream. I could re-count all the impertinent, intrusive, or arrogant questions here, but they're endless and boring and I frankly don't want to give anyone any ideas. What I will say is that, when I mention that something might be a personal question, people tend to say that they're just really curious. They say this in an innocent tone of voice as though surely I can understand, and furthermore, why, I should be grateful. Grateful, I say, that they want to know more about the life and times of the transsexual; grateful that they're not running away shrieking or throwing rotten fruit. If I push the issue and suggest that querying people on their history, former name, surgical status, and so on is rude, my interlocutor gets angry, accuses me of being oversensitive, or asks me if I have something to hide. Which is unfair, and also tiring.

The truth is that I might not mind as much if I didn't understand so well what was going on. I might be willing to believe that there was some sort of innocent educational journey at work every single one of those times, if I hadn't already answered those questions over and over only to discover that each of my questioners was using the information to decide whether or not I was real. I say that my name is Bear, and when I am asked if I have changed my first name to Bear, I say no, it's my middle name. Not real enough. When people learn that my grandmothers still call me Sharon, it's further proof: not the real deal. These judgments are made about surgeries, about hormones, about sexual orientation, and people who ask them—the same people who moments before claimed the need for my tender educational mercies—are now the gender judge and jury.

Transpeople lose a number of things when we transition. We can lose family, friends, jobs, children, lovers, and money. But the most difficult thing for me to lose has been veracity. I was already used to not being real, but now I don't even seem to be trustworthy. I'm not a reliable reporter about my sex or my gender or even my own name; I cannot be trusted to be my own expert. In each of those querying moments, what I am being asked for are details so someone else can make the final decision—am I real yet? So they can decide what they want to call me or how they want to refer to me or if I deserve the pronouns I have requested (and therefore asserted to deserve). I'm only truthful if they decide, after assessing the facts, that my actions mean I deserve the identity that I am claiming. I only get to be real if they say so.

It's tempting to make the comparison to the Velveteen Rabbit, and tidy as well—and you know essayists; we love to wrap up a good metaphor with a pithy ending. Here I just say that I know I'm real, that I believe in it fully, and if I can become real to just one person it's enough to sustain me. But unlike the Velveteen

Rabbit, who was redeemed from death through love but never allowed to be near his love again, it takes more than one person believing in my realness. It takes cultural change. And so this essay doesn't really end as much as it stops. I'll let you know if I ever get more real.

II. *Practice*

I had a long, difficult conversation with my old friend and mentor John last year. I was talking about someone important to me who had a new lover, and I referred to him as her boyfriend. John stopped me mid-sentence to ask, "A transsexual guy?"

I'm afraid I kind of lost my composure. I snapped back, none too kindly, something snotty like, "Are you seriously asking me about the genitals of some dude you don't even know?" and we let the matter drop and went for lunch. But as is so often the case with people to whom we are close, we circled around back to it again in our way, after our feelings had cooled a little, after I was ready to talk to my old friend as a friend and not as a full-time professional gender warrior (which is, or should be, the right of friends). After a few weeks, he sent an email with a chatty first paragraph and then, after a tentative opening, he wrote this:

> At the baggage carousel, I was, indeed, asking about the genitals of someone dating [name redacted]. There are all kinds of reasons why my question was socially problematic, and deserving of a dismissive or indignant response—but your particular indignant response, as I read it, seemed to have as its subtext, "Why on earth should genitals matter in the least?"

I know full well that sex and gender are different things
and I'm well aware of, and fully support, the deconstruc-
tion of those parts of the sex-gender dynamic that are
constructed, which is to say almost all of it. But genitals
seem to matter a lot to people who have them, regardless
of their sex or their gender. Which means, I think, that
they must matter in any discussion of a human relationship between people with genitals.

Okay, genitals are private, and as a rule ought not to be
asked about. But, *but*—when we wish to know or talk
about a person's life and relationships, do we not have to
basically agree on the terms of the discussion in order for
the discourse to have any meaning at all? To the extent
that the LGBTQ community is laboring righteously to
change the terms of these discussions, I'm all for it. I'm
decades past thinking that genitals determine anything,
necessarily. But that's not to say that they don't matter, sometimes a lot. They can't possibly be off the table
entirely, can they? I just don't see how that's possible. The
sex-gender discussion, obviously, is not in a settled or
stable state. As long as that's true, doesn't everything have
to be on the table (as it were) while we sort it out? Which
means, I think, that my question was not as out of line as
your response seemed to suggest.

It's half the problem with old friends, I'm afraid. They really call
you on your shit. And they make it difficult to sidestep the complex parts of the question by dismissing the entire thing on a bad
premise. It's not like answering the questions of a university un-

dergraduate, in which I can address only the parts of the question I want to discuss. On the other hand, with old friends I can talk about things I feel, and ways in which I'm tender, not just what I have studied or can prove. I wrote back:

Okay, that's fair. Here's the thing:

When I identify someone's gender (with a pronoun, name, or other gendered words like "boyfriend") and then someone inquires about genitals, here's the subtext I hear: "Is this person really a man? Help me assess." And that's complicated. Granted, you and I have a long and fairly close history, in a somewhat odd but present way, and so in part I should have been more thoughtful about the fact that you were asking that question in relationship to how it might affect me. I'll take that, and apologize if I was an ass about it. But about gender and genitals, I still have a few thoughts:

Those questions are complicated because it seems to suggest that further interrogation of trans bodies is appropriate, which is a difficult concept. A lot of my work is about saying, hey—here's my gender. Deal with me on the face. If there's some possibility that you might encounter my genitals, we'll deal with that when we get there. And also, it's about creating a space in the world for others to say the same. Asking a transperson about hir sex will always carry a whiff of, "But what are you, *really*?"

It is a lot like asking someone what name they were given

at birth; it's a way of trying to peel someone apart in a way that is intimate or invasive (based, largely, on the relationship between asker and askee). I do not use my first name anymore; no one calls me that except my parents and older relatives. When strangers ask, "What does the S. stand for?" I say, "My first name." When people ask me about my genitals, I invite them to tell me about their own first. Being a display-model transmasculine person is a full-time job, but it does not pay well enough to offer all comers a look into my underpants, metaphorical or otherwise. It's an intimacy, and I reserve the right to reveal it only to my intimates.

So—do genitals matter? Of course. The question for me then becomes—to whom, and why? I talk about my genitals with those people who I may reasonably imagine, through word or deed, have a legitimate interest (a group pretty well limited to my doctor, my therapist, and anyone with whom I have sex). The fact that my genitals are nonstandard for my gender matters to my mechanic or bank teller not at all—they are not interacting with them. Does someone learn more about me if I talk about my parts? Well, maybe. But why do they want to know? How many times in a day do I have to drop my pants for the educational good of others?

Am I defensive about this? Yes, certainly. As a transmasculine person, I experience a lot of poking and prodding at that emotional spot—what are you, really?—and it has become tender in response. So tender that sometimes really perfectly okay questions (like, "will your friend be babymaking with this new guy?") *feel* like the same kind of accusation (Aha! Imposter!) that I more regularly experience.

That's where the "gender crime" part comes in, the sense that I am somehow committing a fraud. Did you follow the Susan Stanton case in Florida? The manager of a small city down there announced her intention to transition from male to female and was fired. Why? Because despite fourteen years service and a sterling record, she was suddenly viewed as "dishonest." They felt they could no longer trust her. She had not been "forthcoming," at which no one should have been surprised, considering what happened, but whatever. Her gender crime made her unfit for service to the city, and they sacked her without delay.

So, it's all charged. And again, I'm sorry—I could have responded better and more thoughtfully to you, and should have. I welcome your questions; I find them thoughtful and interesting. But that's why that's such a tender location of inquiry—people keep hitting it with big sticks.

His reply was a few weeks in coming. By the middle of March, just when I was starting to fear that my response had been alienating, I got this:

You have nothing to apologize for—the world could use more compassionate indignation. I merely noticed your response, which got me thinking, and I thank you for that. And I take all of your points, except one, and maybe half of another one.

The lesser point: Is it possible to interrogate the body without questioning the authenticity of the gender? I think so, because I think that's what I was doing. Of course, I also realize that could easily be taken for a rhetorical dodge—many a respectable bigot sidesteps his own bigotry with a stated desire to "discuss/face things openly" or "see all sides of a question." Righteous pseudo-rationality is very convenient when one is trying to ratify some noxious norm or convention. I don't think this is what I was doing, and of course the bigot never does, so some self-directed skepticism is certainly in order. (For all of us. All the time.)

The larger point. Re: "The fact that my genitals are non-standard for my gender matters to my mechanic or bank teller not at all—they are not interacting with them." Not so! And I realize I consign myself to some neo-Freudian hell the minute I say this, but we are all in some way interacting with each other's genitals all the time, just as we are interacting with all the other aspects of each other that we cannot see but know are there—heart, "heart," brain, mind, digestive organs, soul, etc. Any feeling of kinship or enmity or attraction or caution, however significant or trivial, rests on a platform of knowledge that includes the physical. ("Do I not bleed?") For all of us, all the time. Does that give the bank teller license to inquire about my genitals? Socially, ordinarily, no. But the inquiry is there, and there naturally and necessarily, because we are the same species, whether it's voiced or unvoiced. (And I see that word "naturally" in the preceding sentence, and it's screaming "Delete! Delete! Uncool!" at me, but I'm going to resist deleting it because *I will not* be cowed by a potential connotation, and I do precisely mean "naturally" and not "normally" as the connotation might go. Also because I'm hoping that having triggered your indignation once, your red flags might sit this one out. I hope I've earned that, but if I haven't, if I'm entitling some heteronormative box—I trust you'll kick me out of it.)

And I see that this has big social implications for gender-genital configurations you have termed nonstandard. Okay, they're a complication to the "standard" social platform, but so what? We have to deal with them, hopefully with wisdom and humanity, which is where your life's work tends, may G-d hold you in the palm of hir hand as long as you are willing and able to do it. There's obviously a long way to go, and yes I know the Stanton case, and it's a really bad deal. But our organs can't be taken off the table. They're part of the table, even in the grocery checkout line.

It's lovely to have smart friends. They make you smarter, especially when you've known them for more than half your lifetime, even with time off for good behavior. So I replied:

Right, okay. And for you, who is about a foot smarter and probably a yard more willing to saddle up for variances in the human experience than most people, that'll all probably work in a way that also allows me to have my life. You see? This is a balancing act—how much information do I give, or can I give, and still get though my day? Can the bank teller get a sense of me, in context, enough to do the banking, without knowing about my genitals? Yes. Are they nonetheless at work in some way? Probably also yes, I'll give you that. Maybe especially for me. But where is my responsibility to the bank teller, and where is my responsibility to my own banking chores getting done? Where, for that matter, is my responsibility to my own sense of safety and well-being?

So, theoretically, I am more than willing to take your point, and sign up for the idea that we are all, constantly, interacting with one another's bodies in all their messy, furry, damp, ungainly, brilliant, delicious ways. But also I am not theoretically banking.

In the practical realm, people (about whom I generalize in this Standard American Television Culture) do not react well to things—any things—which are nonstandard. We have a big love affair with normal and abnormal, with normal getting rewarded and abnormal being punished. So then it becomes this intense thing of assessing: how much educating am I willing to do? What's my risk here? How much energy do I have to be a transthing right now? For a while, right before *Butch Is a Noun* came out, I was responding to queries from strangers about my work by saying I had written a book about the history of bananas, because I got overwhelmed with the sheer number of times a day I was being called upon to stop everything and explain what a book titled *Butch Is a Noun* could be about, and stand while I did it under a newly very measuring gendered eye.

And sometimes, like with Susan Stanton, people do not respond well. Especially if they liked me when they thought I was a regular ol' dude, if perhaps a little better spoken than usual—now their own discernment, maybe their own identities, have been called into question. They liked a tranny? A queer tranny? That cannot be—therefore, I must have tricked them (and G-d forbid if they were in any way attracted to me). The quiet "I think you'd better go now" is not a pleasure, no matter when I hear it. So, the larger point is all very well and good—and I can agree, if we keep it theoretical. But on the micro level, where I actually go with my actual genitals to the actual bank? It's one angstrom of progress at a time, and most of it is getting paid for by transfolk, who can least afford it and have the most at stake. Which is why such interrogations of the body, when undertaken by you (or

anyone for whom it is a place of privilege—that is, anyone
whose gender/genital arrangement is standard) should
be approached with the understanding that it is a tender
spot, that even for those of us who walk around in our
bodies more or less just fine there are still a lot of issues
about legitimacy at stake, and if you don't want to trigger
them you'll want to show your willingness to protect that
tender spot in the conversation before you open it (about
which, for the record, we're clear here).

After this email, a lot of time passed. That's not terribly unusual
between John and me; sometimes there are gaps. But then, in
May, I received the following:

Ach. Okay. You're right, of course: we don't live in theory.
Which is why I don't have much patience for what people
tell me they believe—increasingly I feel like beliefs and
actions relate 1:1, which is depressing when you see what
people really do most of the time, though not, thank G-d,
all the time.

And I wish to heck I didn't have to go where I feel I must
go with this, because I care about you so much; your
work, yes, to be sure, but also your tender spots, some of
which I've known about since you were still, to most of us,
a girl.

Suppose, for the sake of discussion, a modicum of decency, intelligence, and mutual respect exists between you

and me, or between you and anyone for that matter. We
engage in discourse. On my side there is appalling privilege and a certain amount of ignorance, in addition to curiosity and the aforementioned decency, etc. There is not,
however, much ambiguity about some aspects of my identity. On your side, in addition to great generosity and the
aforementioned decency, etc., there are widely shared pro-
fessions of identity prostitution, stories about creating and
enjoying warps in the social continuum of gender-normal,
and more clinically, the details of your essay "Tranny
Bladder" over against references a few chapters earlier to
your cock. And even if I hadn't read your book, you met
me in a major airport, in all your gender-jamming glory,
in a sweatshirt emblazoned "Transmasculine."

I'm trying to see why I shouldn't try to figure out what
those things mean, in the most respectful way possible,
which is by asking the person who is saying them. By
asking you. And here's the hard part—what if "I" isn't me,
but someone else. Are the rights and responsibilities of
interrogation contingent on the circumstances? At what
point—and it seems to me there must be a point—must
the choices you have made (above) constrain the choices
you can make re: protection of tender spots?

I feel very ungenerous and not a little queasy as I write
this, because whatever you might be guilty of, I doubt you
are guilty of hypocrisy. And I am constrained by my own
humanity, at the very least, from treading heedlessly on

anyone's tender spot. But haven't I, along with thousands
of others, been warmly and openly invited to consider
your tender spots—indeed, to make ourselves better by
the vicarious habitation of your life on the micro level,
both physical and meta-physical?

I never replied to his email. Mostly I didn't reply because I didn't
know the answer, and I continue not to reply because I still don't
(though it hasn't stopped me publishing the correspondence in a
book, has it?). How much am I inviting these kinds of questions
because I talk about gender and sexuality issues? If I am willing
to take some questions, do I have to take all of them? If I wear
a shirt that reads TRANSMASCULINE, what responsibility am I accepting? If we're likening me to a whore, does the price of my
hire entitle the purchaser to whatever ze wants of me? Or am I
entitled to keep some things private—or, perhaps, to negotiate a
separate price for each? If people have questions, am I responsible
to each and every one of them? If I answer them, am I setting the
example that people can go ahead and ask transfolk whatever they
want, measuring again and again rather than taking us at our
word? Or am I slaking their thirst to understand in such a way
that will keep them from asking anyone else?

I don't know. I also don't know how much these questions are
built on our experience, and how much on our personalities. But I
must uncomfortably confess that I leave the conversation in much
the same place that I began it. I have great respect for John, and
great belief in his empathy, but I can still feel my hackles rising
uncomfortably when someone starts their interrogation, however
friendly, always understanding that in some way the underlying

question is, "Are you real or not?" On the other hand, I already know that sometimes—as woo-woo as I know this sounds—sometimes if I lean into other people a little bit and offer them my trust before I expect theirs, things can go better than I expect. Which, for a worn-out tranny warrior who spends way more time in airports than with old friends, is kind of a nice thing to be able to hold on to.

It Only Takes a Minute, II

There is, in fact, nothing wrong with me. Or with my husband or with any of my friends, and though I know the Gender Identity Disorder diagnosis-and-treatment model has served some people well over time, I find it harder and harder to get on board. So I apologize for not reacting more warmly to your explanation of how you got your workplace to cover your surgery and medical leave. I know it's a huge relief for you, but I'm conflicted. Glad you got what you need, worried that it's not a good precedent.

In Wisconsin, at a hotel happy hour for business travelers, I accept a glass of a nice white and sit on a low couch. I'm facing a good-looking, sturdy blonde woman with her briefcase and binder set on the seat beside her. "Nothing wrong with free wine," I remark casually. "I tried to get my husband to come down, but he's watching the game," she replies. I grin, and say, "I don't think my husband's ever watched a game in his life," even though we're not married yet. Suddenly she likes me a lot better, and we talk and drink wine for an hour. I remain unsure if I was redeemed as a straight woman or a gay man.

At my wedding, Zev and Turner are taking one of my grandmothers, in her wheelchair, from the place where we were taking photos to the tent under which the wedding will be held. Making conversation, Zev asks my grandmother which side she's on, meaning: my mother's mother, or my father's mother? Grandma puffs up and announces, "The bride's." Turner and Zev make sure not to dissolve into giggles until they are safely out of earshot.

My nearest-by Starbucks, purveyors of the iced grandé caramel double espresso that writes books, employs a cadre of young stylish white girls and one teensy gay boy. My low-level flirting has apparently caused some conversation: one of the girls murmurs quietly to me as she hands over the magic potion that the tallest girl and the little boy were *both* wondering if I was single. I grin and say I'm married, which I think answers the question. She looks vexed.

When I see queer-lookin' people out and about, especially while traveling, I like to at least smile and nod. In Nashville, at the supermarket, I see two short-haired tattooed women standing close together, and grin at them, friendly-like. One glares and the other sneers at me, and I make a quick escape down the frozen foods aisle. Either I have misread them, or they've misread me. Anyone have suggestions for how to tell which it is?

The Field Guide to Transmasculine Creatures

Gender is complicated. I'm here to tell you. I have worked on nearly every other essay here before this one, because although gender is complicated, writing it into understandability is part of why they let me publish books. The issue is, there is no part of the genderverse quite so complicated for me to write about as the questions and arguments around who is a butch and who is a transguy and how I came to this conclusion (full points are not awarded unless I show my work, like on math exams). Evidently, I have to be a grownup and write about the most tender and dreaded topic of my identity universe, having already far outstripped the once-deadly taboo of butches getting fucked, which hardly anyone thinks is even news anymore (although it's taken the entirety of some people's active sexual lives to come to this realization).

The bigger problem is that I just don't know what to tell you. I know it's important. I talk about it all the time, get email about it every day, hear from people existing in a state of anguish because they don't know what to do. Should they transition? Have they transitioned already and they just haven't named it that? Or how do they get people to recognize that they *have* transitioned, and stop inviting them to women's events? How big is the difference between Butch and Transsexual Man. Are there middle grounds? Where are *those* defined? Could I please send a map, or failing that, a chart or a graph?

I just don't think it's that easy.

There are a few things I find myself trying to remember to

point out rather often. Most of them have to do with assumptions about what words mean, what experiences mean, and what kinds of things either of those permit or preclude, which is often decided as though they are absolute. Perhaps the first topic related to the Border Wars I want to take up is: please stop treating gender as though it were a set menu.

Gender is an à la carte arrangement, even though the macroculture rarely realizes this and doesn't usually act accordingly. We are all, I firmly believe, in charge of our own genders. We can choose to have the final say about what they do or do not include, and we can make changes to those things if we want to and decide we can afford them (afford, that is, in terms of cash, or relationships, or values, or the approval of those in our lives). But because the cultural message we're all steeped in is that gender is a fixed arrangement, even the most politically progressive among us—and I include myself in this—can forget or overlook how very variable gender can be when we want it to be.

Further, genders that are unusual, nonstandard, mix-n-match, or new to us are just as valid as the ones we're more accustomed to. My conversations with people who are just beginning to understand and include transsexual and transgender people in their plans or programs lean heavily on this. For them, the very fact of a transsexual who is a real student at their school or client of their agency can be new and surprising. But for queers and transfolk, who have institutionalized an additional set of queerly normative genders, it can sometimes be difficult to hear that we, too, must expand. If butch daddies want to crochet, if twinkly ladyboys are sometimes tops in bed, if burly bears can do BDSM play as little girls, if femme fatales build bookcases in their spare time, these things, too, are not just good but great. They bring us, I believe, wonderful news: news that gendered options can continue to explode, that the chefs in the kitchen of gender are creating new and imaginative specials every day. That we, all of us, are the chefs. Hi. Have a whisk.

Unfortunately, it seems that we are more likely to decide that these people, and their genders, are secretly fraudulent. That after all this gender mixing, all this firm and sweet belief that a female-bodied person can be called Rocky and be ferocious as a hurricane, we cannot quite make the next step and let Rocky also like to needlepoint. So many of us will go so far as to accept a nontypical gender-and-sex pairing—but only if the gender is uncomplicated.

Maybe yours is relatively straightforward, no pun intended. And that's fine. There is plenty of room for *everyone's* gender in the New Gendered Order. Mine, which is as messy as chocolate-chip cookies made by a pack of eight-year-olds, and yours, which may be a perfect soufflé, all ingredients combined in elegant harmony. Also fine: everyone else's gender. Not to extend the cookery metaphor forever, but fusion cookery is popular for a reason. Macaroni and cheese is delicious with truffle oil and a little blue cheese mixed into the sauce.

And so, when we start to look for the line of demarcation between the butch and the transman, the complex parts can be hard to sort. Certainly there are people who are perfectly easy to categorize—they'll tell you right away who and what they are. They've chosen, invested in their choices, and that is the end of that. I am thinking, as I write, of transmen I know who feel as though they have always been male but whose bodies were a little slower catching up, is all. They are men of male experience, not butches. Many were never butch identified. Many are rather tired of having it implied that they were. Some transguys have nothing whatsoever to do with butch flight. It turns out that masculinity in female-bodied people is even more complex than we have been assuming all along.

Which, I suppose, is why everyone is so desperate for the Field Guide; the magical series of taxonomic determinations that will tell you what exactly you are, or are dealing with. Then, I hear in people's requests, then I will know what I am dealing with. Then I will know what pronoun to use. Then I will know who I am permitted to be attracted to. Then I will not have to have my shirts re-monogrammed.

(It's worth noting that while I was swanning around the house trying to remember the name for the chart-thingum you use to figure out what kind of bug you found, Ishai commented that it rather suggested a little boxful of butches with pins through them. This, of course, is not at all what I want, neither the fixed-ness nor, you know, the deadness. This is the biggest problem with classifying things; a classifier often cannot know exactly what they've got until the subject is dead.)

It's not that I'm unsympathetic to the desire for security, for understanding, for tidy boxes. It's just that I'm not your guy. I'm against categorization for a hundred reasons, not the least of which is: as soon as you make a list of the possibilities, you're guaranteed to have left someone *off* the list, which will either piss them off or make them feel invisible, or both. By declining to make a list, by refusing to weigh in on who is really or isn't really a what, now, I am not just protecting my own ass but also trying to protect other people's hearts. Who wants to hear that they're not on the Comprehensive List? Who wants to be told that they cannot imagine their way into a new gender, that they have to choose one out of the book?

When we live in a world that leaves only the tiniest sliver of room for the least complicated among us, it's difficult to find a place for all our complexities. I am afraid that it pushes us to leave our genders unexplored, and I am pretty sure that it does not allow us to express them in all the ways we would prefer. As it goes with many things, it's easy to be afraid of genders that seem dangerous, unusual, or even merely new.

I find it easier to talk about this topic when I can remember that we are all mostly afraid, because I have great compassion for even myself in that. And for femmes who have loved butches since forever, cut the hair of tender warriors in their kitchens because it wasn't always safe to go to the barbershop since forever, treasured the toughness of outlaws who have made lives beyond the bounds of acceptance forever, and are now watching their worlds get smaller. For butches who first worked hard to figure out how to become acceptable to greater society, and then when that was a dismal failure recreated themselves into genders that gave them access to a life, friends, and love, and then could no longer stay there. For masculinely gendered people who are still, however old they are, not sure how to make sense of what they want and need, how to navigate the world, how to stay safe and feel warmed and get enough of what they need to survive, and then work toward thriving. For transmen who slap the hands of people trying to span the distance between butch and transman within their arms' length, not out of dislike of butches, but because their identities depend in some part on making that distance much more than a body's length, much more than a short hop.

This seems like a digression, but isn't: My parents used to be very upset about my masculine gender expression. They tried a lot of things to get me to be girlier, some of them not very nice. Now, they do not appear to care one way or another about my level of girliness. It has been suggested that they've gotten more accustomed to my masculinity, but I don't think that's quite it. Instead, I think, they were so diligent at first because they were afraid. They didn't know anyone who looked and acted like me. No one in their universe, no one with a partner and kids and friends and a profession was like me. And so they tried to police me into being more like someone they could imagine a good future for. As it began to develop that I could have all those things and be just as faggoty a butch/dandy/queer as I am, they seemed to care a lot less. Now we don't even talk about it. It's just, for the most part, how I am.

I think we're all guilty of letting our fears drive our actions. I realize now, dug deep into the question of butch or FTM or transmasculine and who's a what, that we get activated in the exact same way my nice, straight parents do: out of fear. We're worried that we'll make a mistake, or that we already have, and that the consequences will be more than we can manage. That we'll take the wrong path, say the wrong thing, get a crush on the wrong person, be identified wrongly, have the wrong expectations, make the wrong move—all of it. And at the risk of answering the same question the same way over and over: it's not a fucking binary. It would be easier for a lot of people if it were, but it just bloody well ain't, and nothing any of us does can make it that way. Please take a deep breath.

Or, better yet, how about this: be glad. Be glad that there's so much play, so much slip and slide, in queer genders. Be glad to have an opportunity to learn more and do better. Be glad that there are so very many variations of the transmasculine body to enjoy—your own or someone else's. Be glad that we, the butches and boys and bois and transguys and transsexual men and FTMs and MTMs and trannyfags and Studs and Aggressives and all of us now have the agency to speak about our own lives, use our own words, and give our own experiences our own names. Instead of wishing for the Field Guide, be glad to live in the beautiful chaos of each of us finding our way into our own gendered menu, our own identity, and our own name for it, which—if you will just love us while we do this complex and fragile part—we will kiss into your mouth with such gratitude when we're through.

I'm Just Saying

I'm just saying: *I have never really felt like a girl* is not the same as *I have always felt like a boy*. I mention this because when I have these tortuous inner conversations about how I may yet need to change my body and whether (and in what way) I am prepared to invest myself in the destination model of transition, I have to keep reminding myself of this important thing. It's disheartening, in a way, because you'd think that someone who makes a living kicking at the gender binary would do a little better with this, frankly. But no. The ways of the gender binary are often dark and never pleasant; it can and will suck you right back in to its uncompromising orbit without remorse.

When I look at myself in the mirror, I am looking for handsome, never pretty. I don't think I was ever pretty, even once, as hard as I tried to fake it, and I did. For the benefit of my family, for my own safety, for camouflage or comfort or whatever reasons at whatever moments, I worked at it. More than just the odd once. I still have the long, wild earrings I wore to make earrings feel like an all-right choice, and I am pretty sure that somewhere in a bucket in the old bathroom at my folks' house are the green mascara and copper lipstick I tried too. It always felt wrong, in the way that people talk about the ineffable wrongness of their early lives. I was never good at it. I never felt right; never felt like a girl.

I suppose I don't know what Girl feels like, or what Woman does. I know that when I want to I can shape my voice into Woman over the phone, and I know what that feels like mostly because of the response I get. I sound educated, polished, and professional. There's a silk I can bring to it, a way of making my words flow and ride that feels womanly to me, different from the firm-ended sentences of my more natural masculine discourse. That voice feels to me like it seems Woman ought to, as much grace as power, as much music as lyrics, and maybe that's the result of having been raised up by high femmes, but that's fine with me. That voice, she comes easily and feels natural in my mouth.

But nothing about Woman ever felt natural in my body. I have catalogued and discussed the ways of this and theorized about why, but at the end of the day my form is as broad and unyielding as the things I was compared to, and not kindly, as a child: a Mack truck, a bull elephant, a linebacker. I can remember with hot shame the moments in which adults of my childhood said those things to me, and I knew they weren't compliments. I also, however, know this: in my twenties I was asked to dance as part of a performance, and repeated to the great and talented Peggy Shaw what the dance captain of my adolescence had said about me, that I had "all the natural grace of a rampaging bull elephant." I said it as a way to get myself off the hook, but Peggy, being a tall and broad-beamed butch thing herself, looked at me seriously and asked if I had ever seen a rampaging bull elephant. I had not. She shook her head slowly and said that to see so large a thing move so determinedly and so fast was a particular kind of grace all its own, and could not be denied. Maybe, she opined, an elephant's grace was exactly the kind I had, and there was nothing in the world wrong with that.

But I haven't always felt like a Boy or wanted to be a Man. Maybe that's the feminist I am, an identity and word I claim even though I sometimes find I don't enjoy other people who also claim it. Maybe I am too suspicious of the offices of manhood. But really, beyond all the theorizing and ex post facto explanations, I don't know what a Man feels like. I cannot see that sure, certain thing that other people I love and trust seem to see, clear and true—that thing of manhood that is a destination many people feel excited about. I have nurtured in myself a masculinity I feel comfortable in and pleased about, but sometimes my choices, in trying to live up to Man, feel just as alien as my early attempts at Girl did.

Part of me understands that these things are about culture, stereotype, and archetype; not all girls wear mascara and not all boys spit and swear. I adore all of the small children in my life, and I hope that one of the things I am able to provide for them (besides love and endless repetitions of their favorite let's-pretend scenarios) is plenty of encouragement to ignore the forces of gender and do what they feel called to. I want them to feel encouraged and supported in their genders, and their choices about gender—in ways I do not. I want them to assume that whatever they feel like is perfectly good, and that if it feels like boy to them, then it is; likewise girl. Perhaps most of all, I want them to feel that they and only they are the absolute and unassailable experts in this regard, that no matter what anyone else thinks or says, they are right, right, right about their gender, and then right some more, a big enough and sturdy enough right to carry them past anyone's protestations.

I catch myself even now—in an essay, for G-d's sake, about resisting the gender binary—resorting to binary, fish-or-fowl thinking. We're raised on it, fed it and simmered in it, and all of our language supports it and recreates it. Saying even one sentence about gender without buying into the gender binary requires so many circuitous locutions and scare quotes that I get exhausted. Even me, and I do not mean "even me" because I am so very fabulous or so unusually smart, but after daily battle with gendered language one does build up some endurance, and so when I say it I mean, *even me who hauls this particular bucket of water every damn day.*

There are more locations than girl and boy, man and woman. Decamping from one does not have to mean climbing into another. There's plenty of space in between, or beyond the bounds, or all along and across the plane or sphere or whatever of gender, and it is entirely okay to say, "I do not like being a girl, and so I shall be a boy." But it must also be okay to say, "I do not like being a girl, so I shall set about changing what it means to be a girl," and, yes, okay to say, "I do not like being a girl, and so I shan't." Totally okay. Not always easy, not always tidy, not always something one can briefly explain—but can you say it? Of course you can. Of course.

But would it be nice to have a destination? Well, yes.

Maybe that's just me. Maybe it's my Virgo, Jewboy nature talking, wanting to know where we're going, when we are expected to arrive, for how long we will be staying, what transportation we'll be taking and what it costs and how frequently it runs. I make my husband crazy in this particular way all the time on vacations.

It's true I have never felt like a girl, but I have felt like a Bear. I moved into that name lock, stock, and barrel the moment it was given to me, and I have used it whenever gender was demanded of me. Are you a boy or a girl? I'm a Bear. Will you be a Mama or a Papa? I'll be a Bear. "I'm not that kind of Bear," I have said teasingly or seriously, and more than once. When people ask me if I'm a Bear as in *grrr* or a Bear as in teddy, I smile and say, "Yes." Bears are large and fuzzy, which I am, and can be forbidding or tender; me too. I have the Bear hug. I know what Bear feels like, and when I don't I can decide that since I am the Bear, however I am in a moment is the right way for me to be. I can decide this without particular concern since there are so few cultural expectations for a gender of Bear, so I feel utterly free to inhabit it just as I like, to create a whiff of the experience I hope to encourage in the children of whom I am fond. I feel at home in my name. Using it as a gender, and sometimes as a sexuality, is a bonus.

I don't always talk about myself as a Bear. I use boy words to talk about myself too, especially in terms of my size. Fat Boy and Big Fella feel friendly and familiar; they feel warm, unlike other terms, and I understand that this is because, culturally, we have a whole different relationship to fat in women than we do in men. When given a choice between being Some Guy and Some Girl, I always pick Some Guy, and I have learned to accept and enjoy Buddy, Chief, and so on as useful and appropriate nominatives in no-name-given situations. In the end I am a masculine being, an opener of doors and a wearer of boots and a relinquisher of bus seats and a person with a relationship to my tailor. In this masculine light, in moments without a lot of opportunity to explain and discuss my gendered choices built in, I am willing and cheerful to be Some Guy.

Regrettably, the results of this do not always match my choices. There is no space for "masculine-being, female-anatomy, feminist-consciousness, politically and sexually queer, transgressively gendered" to become specific and recognized in many locations of daily life, such as the public bathroom or the honorific attached to my bank account or frequent-flyer membership. To these, I take the gender-free option when there is one. I talk about gender nonspecific pronouns like I was being sponsored by them. With only slight guilt, I assign myself the honorific of Dr and use the Family or Accessible washrooms when they're available to avoid further, external gendered confusion. When they are not available, I generally choose the expedient of using whatever name, honorific, or facility seems safest in the situation; usually the masculine, since, well, see above.

And the result can be . . . confusing. Not to me, since I am in here, making the choices (in the same way the driver doesn't get car sick). But living in a location of gender that's complicated may cause staring, upset, difficult conversations, hostility, and worry far more often than it causes curiosity or flirting or delight. When I discuss my choices, I am often asked why I would want to do that—and to be clear, I mean that compassionate and gender-savvy people ask this. We are not counting the votes of the hateful, for whom the polls will always be closed on this topic. I mean that time and again, people who are prepared to understand and accept and include transsexual people want to know why I could not be transsexual: change my name, take hormones, have chest surgery (at least), claim my identity as a man, and be done with it. Which seems both clearer and also easier, it's true.

It's a reasonable question. Being transsexual, while not exactly a walk in the park, is a destination-based mode of gender and tends to be relatively straightforward: I used to be this known, recognized, approved thing, and now I am that known, recognized, approved thing. You already know the rules for this class of person. Adjust yourself accordingly. And most people, even those who might not necessarily be delighted by it, kind of get it and can get on board and will, unless they are invested in proving some kind of bullying "I don't believe in you" point. Certainly this is easier, as most transsexuals will tell you, with new people who don't have to adjust to a transsexual history. People who used to know them under a former name and pronoun pose a different set of questions. But even still, even when people are being mean or stupid, at least there are answers to their questions, you know? I'm a woman now, so you can call me Cheryl and refer to me as she or you can piss off. Simpler.

In my bio, I refer to myself as a gender-jammer, a word I stole and modified from the term "culture-jammer," which refers to those people who make their point about the cultural ills they perceive by publicly enacting an exploration of an institution or hegemony. They usually do it with humor and playfulness, which I enjoy, and let a little light and air into the kinds of things we accept without question. I can do this, be a gender-jammer, because my nontraditional kind of work as a writer and performer makes a lot of room for it. People who are lawyers or consultants or schoolteachers currently have far fewer choices about how they embody their genders, and so my self-employed status as an artist and cultural worker gives me great privilege to be a little weird, in the way we expect of our "creative types." For which I am grateful. Being a well-employed freak with a good education means that I can use all the space not currently occupied by Boy and Girl if I want to, and see what I enjoy and where it might inspire me. Being a homesteader on the landscape of gender is, in some ways, a pretty good deal.

Am I sure I'll always be here? No. I know far too many people who, well into their middle or later years, have finally come to terms with their own genders or have been worn down by the gender expectations of the world in which they live or some combination of that and other things, and they have changed sexes, medically or socially or both. But for now, I am clear, and I have made a choice: I am not, and have never felt like a girl, that's true, and I'm not a woman at all. But neither was I a boy, and I may never be a man. That's how it is over here. I'm just saying.

Passing the Word

I have started to really dislike the word *passing*. I resent it, and my resentment has blossomed fully, if you can imagine some sort of carnivorous and tentacular flower. At this point even the whiff of it makes me cranky, because it has come to represent a particular kind of backwardness in thinking about gender that, to further torment the horticultural metaphor, really frosts my pumpkin. And because I spend so much of my time talking and thinking about questions of gender, someone seems to need to talk to me about passing every day.

Passing, you know: "I pass as a man almost all the time." "Sometimes I pass as a girl, but only until I speak." "One hundred percent passable." It's how we talk about the way a transsexual or transgender person is seen in the world: are they being seen and recognized as their identified and expressed gender? They *pass*. No? Then they *do not pass*. Passing is one of the few words in the transgender lexicon that's not a medical-legacy word. We did ever so much better with this one: it's a racist-legacy word, a legacy of the time when Africans were kidnapped from their homeland to be enslaved in the Americas. If you're not familiar with this, a hierarchy of race developed in which the lighter your skin was, the more attractive and intelligent you were considered, and someone quite light-skinned could sometimes *pass* for white and live in white society. Even as I write this, I snort and sigh and shake my head, thinking, okay. I know I am a word geek. But could we not do any better?

Passing is a word loaded with problems, all of which you may rest assured I will complain about before we're done here, but by far the biggest for me is that it assigns all the responsibility for other people's experience or understanding of a particular person's gender to . . . the person in question. Not the people doing the observing, but the observed. It is your job, the word *passing* communicates, and, what's more, your solemn responsibility to create a presentation of gender that conforms well enough to the prevailing standards of whatever context you find yourself in to call forth from onlookers the gender attribution you desire. Like transpeople need more work to do.

If this does not occur, you have failed; when it does you have succeeded. Not just that, but in the matrix of many transsexual treatment programs those verb forms become their nounal counterparts: if you do not *pass*, you are a failure. If you do, you are a success. Successes may have access to hormones, surgeries, legal remedy with regard to documents, and other such interventions as they require, as a reward for having played the game well. Failures are sent home in disgrace, and this is marketed as the natural way of things. Obviously, the thinking goes, someone who is really and truly a transsexual would be able to make a visual, corporeal case for hirself instinctively (or perhaps with a little time spent with Dr Google), but certainly there are no medical interventions to teach you how. If you cannot do it on your own, you're a failure.

To be a success on the transmasculine spectrum, one must begin by gaining some measure of expertise in, if not mastery over, enough psychology, anthropology, gender studies, and improvisational theater to create and constantly modify a gender presentation that seems male enough. Merely being masculine, and even knowing yourself to be absolutely and utterly a man, will not be enough if you cannot also deepen your voice, comport yourself in a stereotypically masculine fashion, and create the right appearance. If your authentic masculinity is a little faggoty, you probably cannot express it until you've had chest surgery and grown a beard or at least a good crop of stubble. And though this racist-legacy word is not, technically, a medical-legacy word, it is nonetheless frequently adopted by doctors, for if you can do all of these things, if you can pass—then, yes, they will let you be a man. Because, of course, what you think or feel or need has much less to do with it than the opinion of someone with medical training. Clearly.

Carrying on with what has now certainly become a rant, I would also like to discuss the connotations of deception or trickery that come with the word *pass*; the whiff of sneakiness it carries. I can join other brilliant thinkers and write about the myth of the deceptive transsexual until my fingers fall off from hitting the keys too hard, but not nearly as many people will eventually read this essay as will hear from or about a transperson *passing*. As what, may I ask? Does no one else hear the echoes of *passing herself off* or *passing a bad check*? (Ironically, this was the very crime that led to the eventual execution of Brandon Teena.) This construction of *passing* is the tertiary definition of the word, but nevertheless, transpeople have been saddled with it. The addition of the word "as" makes inherent in the phrase the comparison between the then and the now, between the "natural" and the "constructed." When we talk about passing, however much we may mean it in a neutral or even positive way, I wonder and worry about how many of these lexical hangers-on are also making the trip. The loss of that certain personal veracity that transpeople face may have something to do with the fact that every time we talk about how we are in the world—how we legitimately and (mostly) authentically are—we use a word that comes embedded with a question of legitimacy.

And, while we're at it, legitimately what, exactly? While we are busy sticking transpeople with the burden of proof in every single arraignment in the court of public opinion, we simultaneously fail to examine the nature of that court. It is all very well indeed, as North Americans, to imagine that we immutably and everlastingly know things about gender, but any anthropologist worth a pencil can tell that you we don't know a damn thing. That gendered cues change radically according to cultural context, particularly in terms of race, economic class, religious background, ethnicity, sexual orientation, and ability status. No one likes to mention this, because it threatens to interfere with our sense that gender is knowable, definable, and absolute, but, in fact, gender cues are not read in the same way everywhere. Leaving aside even some of the more fabulous examples (because I fear they exoticize cultures that are less well understood by westerners), consider the legion of heterosexual and gender-normative German boys strolling the *strasse* in pink or purple socks and Birkenstocks (yes, at the same time). Or the masculine men of Montreal, who greet everyone, including one another, manfully, with a kiss on each cheek, or the farm women of northern Maine who wear blue jeans and flannel shirts from L.L. Bean and are considered perfectly and precisely gender-normative for their time and place. If you moved either of the above groups into Manhattan or Chicago you would almost certainly conclude that you were in a gay bar (because North Americans reflexively map non-normative gender expression onto queer sexual orientation) and would quite likely begin to speculate on the genders of some of the patrons.

Why is this a problem? It's not, as long as the socks stay in Germany and the farmers in Maine and the kisses in Montreal. But when those people—entirely Normal within their cultural contexts, absolutely cisgendered in their personal identities— arrive in Chicago or Boston, their genders may well be read as suspect, as Other. And the same is true of transpeople. Can you imagine a transwoman from that farming community in northern Maine meeting a physician from South Carolina? Each has hir own idea of what a woman looks like or does or needs to be; each has a clear mental map of how femininity is achieved and maintained. Each idea is, again, entirely culturally correct and totally valid within a context. But they conflict.

So who do we declare the winner? The transwoman, because she has authenticity on her side? The doctor, for having a medical degree? Do we hew to the demands of the American ethos and privilege the privileged, awarding the passing points to the person of higher economic-class status? How would this transwoman *pass*? Perhaps more importantly, and more to the point of my everlasting problem with this word: for whom or by whom would she pass?

(And no fair mumbling about most-people-and-most-places, either. If nothing less than my life, my wellness, to say nothing of my ability to get medical or legal intervention, should I want it, are at stake, and the entire burden of making myself acceptable falls to me alone, then I think I can expect a little consistency, can I not?)

It seems clear to me that this *passing* concept is not really viable at all, certainly not for actual people. It may have worked in a limited way for a minute, as long as all such medical and social transactions took place among people whose cultural contexts and demographic locations were all pretty tidily lined up (or so vastly disparate that those with privilege were free to exoticize and disenfranchise freely). And even with that, the word *passing* always carried with it the strong aroma of exactly what some people think about transfolk. It suggests that they are passing themselves off as something they are not, that there is something undeniably deceptive about them; that there is something superficial or merely cosmetic about our identified and/or expressed genders. But now what do we do? Perhaps even more importantly: now what do we *say*?

My suggestion is that we put the burden where it belongs: on the observer. Imagine a construction of language that, rather than reinforcing an idea of transgender or transsexual people as creating a falsehood, supported the notion that our genders are perfectly natural and inherently truthful. For that to be the case, however, some blame needs to be assigned in cases of disagreement (and no one will allow me to just blame the media culture and its great love affair with the binary, regrettably). I say we assign it to the cisgendered. Rather than talking about who *passes*, let us instead talk about who *reads*.

"They read me as a man." See how this works? That sentence assigns responsibility to the person or people doing the seeing, the reading, rather than further objectifying the object of the gaze. Not just that, but in the sentence it is not clear what the speaker's identified gender or sex assigned at birth is. It could be, in that person's eyes, either a successful or a failed attempt by someone else at correctly parsing their gender, but the onus is on someone other than the speaker. The actions of bystanders, rightly and reasonably, do not reflect on the transperson in question (though, of course, they may affect hir). The idea that someone is attempting to pull some sort of gendered fast one does not make the transition from a sentence constructed with *passing* to a sentence constructed with *reading*; nor is there any sense of endeavor. In no way does the language indict the efforts of the person being read; they are more or less what they are in somewhat the same way a book is what it is—engaging or boring, quick or slow—and these things are understood to be in the eye of the beholder. This is why we have Amazon rankings and reviews on *librarything.com* as opposed to, say, a governmental assessment and eternal branding with the result. Ahem.

I am always in favor of better language: more compassionate, more precise, more lyrical, more aspirational. When we continue to use the word *pass*, we continue to hamper ourselves by endlessly repeating a narrative of deception, not to mention the legacy of racism, the cultural arrogance, and the spectacular level of objectification it brings with it. I do not believe we need this, and what's more I do not believe it's good for us. I would rather move the burden back where it belongs, to the observer, the person whose cultural lens and personal locations on so many axes are in so many ways the day-to-day deciders of how a person is read. To be read is something that happens to all people and carries none of the stigmas attached to its new or old meaning; it is also done by all people, and is not a special test applied only to hapless trannies with the temerity to leave our houses. What is more, maybe most important: passing is fleeting, tricksy, and temporary. But what it takes or means to read depends, rightly and righteously, entirely on who's doing it.

Not Getting Killed, with Kindness

This morning, as I was getting a cup of coffee around the corner, someone asked me whether I was raised in this country. I am sometimes asked what planet I'm from, or even whether I was born in a barn, but this question hasn't come up much. I replied that I was, and wondered why she'd asked. My English is unaccented, my general comportment doesn't seem to suggest foreignness; I wasn't listening to French-language hip-hop on my iPod. She said, with some surprise, that she'd wondered because I was so polite, which she does not associate with Americans. Nodding and grinning, I shrugged, thanked her for the compliment, and said what I usually say in such situations: "I was raised right."

That's true, but it's a half-truth. It is true that I was raised by parents who, whatever their strengths or faults may have been, placed a very high premium on being courteous and friendly. They taught me to say, "May I please," as though it were a single word, and to say, "Thank you," early and often. I learned by example that taking the time to say, "Good morning," to inquire how someone's day is progressing and to actually listen to the answer, go a long way in making one's world a nicer place in which to live. And I internalized a basic understanding of the concept that one gives respect in order to get respect; that it is the height of self-centeredness to assume that anyone will treat me respectfully if I don't treat them in the same way, and that this is true for anyone I encounter in my life, no matter what social status that person's job might seem to confer upon hir. That, in fact, those distinctions are themselves at the heart of American-style rudeness—the idea that the person who makes me a cup of coffee does not deserve to be called Sir and thanked politely absolutely as much as the university president who is about to decide if I get a gig or not.

I wish I could say that I have continued practicing politeness as it was taught to me solely out of a deep sense of respect for all other people until they prove themselves otherwise. I would like to be a person who, for no other reason than coming from a whole-hearted place of honoring the divinity in all beings, treats everyone around me exactly as I believe we all deserve. I'd like to say that, but it isn't quite true. I have to confess to an ulterior motive. If I'm being honest, the truth is that I am courteous and friendly to everyone I meet, or at least I try to be, because I want them to like me *before* they notice what a freak I am and try to punish me for it.

I recognize that, on the page, this sounds like hyperbole, and in some ways it is. I do not, in general, feel myself to be in any immediate danger of being sucker-punched by the receptionist at my doctor's office or roughed up by an associate professor of modern literature (though the receptionist at my shrink's office, Trish, is a no-nonsense Southern girl who could clearly lay a smackdown if she cared to). But I never trust myself to make such judgments, and so I make the decision to exercise my particular brand of Nice Boy courtesy in all situations.

Also, there are other considerations, gradations between completely accepting and hiding a baseball bat behind hir back. The ways of punishment can be so subtle I never know about them, never know what I could have had or done if I hadn't been so threatening to look at. What visible outlaw has never been sweetly told that the job was filled, the apartment was rented, the manager was out for the day, that no substitutions were allowed, that all bags must be checked, that the thirty-four-dollar fee still applied even for a seventeen-cent overdraft? I don't know any. We all pay a price for looking different in any way, from my thirteen-year-old niece, the goth princess whose typing teacher sent her to the principal's office to be disciplined the day she appeared at school with pink hair, to my former students, elite-level athletes in the basketball program whose great size and black skin were so anomalous in our smallish New England town that bank clerks played a passive-aggressive game of Not It in order to avoid having to help them. It was in talking with them about their experiences in the public eye that I started to recognize how much my reflexive politeness and gregarious ability to make a few minutes of social chat with nearly anyone had smoothed my way: I eventually escorted my students to my local branch of the bank and introduced them to the three tellers with whom I was acquainted from my own visits there, and they had no problems after that. They, too, had moved from Those People to someone individual and knowable.

As someone who moves through the world being visibly queer, visibly beyond the bounds of the traditional gender binary, being someone individual and knowable is one of the most powerful tools I have. I am aware that I am always—whether I want to be or not—an ambassador for my people. At the very least, I am aware that this is always a possibility. And it is a possibility I take seriously. If someone is encountering a queer person, or a readably transgendered person, for the first or even the tenth time, I would like that person to remember me as being, really, perfectly all right. Not freakish or lecherous or miserable or rude, not anything but moving easily in my world, giving respect and hoping to receive it in return.

In the best moments, a brief conversation gives me a chance to close the gaps caused by ignorance a little further and make pleasant, small-talky conversation about the weather or the dog or some minor local event. Something that further underscores the idea that although some parts of my life are and will continue to be radically different from theirs—and I am not a proponent of the We're Just Like You Except for What We Do in Bed philosophy—it is nonetheless true that in some ways our lives are not always all that dissimilar. I, too, walk my dog and worry about the consistency of his poop—even if I may share my dog with my queer femme ex-wife who maintains a separate household, which is next door to her best friend who is my former lover and owned boy and also a transsexual to boot. I, too, struggle to remain calm and good-natured while making alternate arrangements to compensate for air travel delays, even if I am flying to Milwaukee to perform my queer, transgendered, Jewish solo theater piece, which is my sole source of income, and the major source of my consternation is coordinating airport pickup for my lover from Pittsburgh, who is flying in separately and meeting me at the airport (and is also a transsexual, to boot).

I do not always reveal these conditions explicitly (though I have certainly been known to), but I tend to think that they are assumed, if not specifically then generally. Your average heterosexual, Christian mother of three is probably not looking at me and assuming that our lives are full of points of intersection. And let's face it, we're all wary of what we don't know or don't understand. So my working theory is that whatever opportunity I have to close that gap a little bit is a way of activism, as valid as the work I do standing up and lecturing about gendery things and probably, in the final analysis, with a higher success rate. I'm trying to demystify queers and transfolk, in both cases, trying to be approachable and basically regular, not afraid to laugh at myself and not afraid to answer hard questions, but also just as glad to sit and talk about the designated-hitter rule or whether *Law & Order: SVU* is better than the original *Law & Order* series. If I'm going to be someone's introduction to LGBTQ folks in any kind of setting (and I assure you that there are people who shudder miserably at that idea), I want to use the opportunity to be someone they can like even though some things in our lives are very, very different. I want to move us from Those People to "that person I always see walking his dog who lets my daughter give it treats," or "that person who gave me the name of that great Bosnian restaurant in Saint Louis." I will happily settle, any day, for, "I don't know, that transgender came and talked to our class, and he or she or whatever didn't seem so weird."

But the ways of gender are fickle, and on some days I become aware of the fact that I am not being read as queer or gender transgressive but as a perfectly ordinary boy, white and at least middle-class and ostensibly heterosexual in my jeans and boots. Truth be told, I'm always tempted by those opportunities. It would be so easy to slouch, scowl, mumble, "Gimme a turkey sammich on rye," let doors bang shut behind me. I could spit and swear and jerk my chin to indicate what I want without even saying a word, certainly not please or, at any further stage, thank you. Not only would it be easy, it would probably help me to continue being read as a boy, as my reflexive politeness in those moments is in fact the most transgressive thing about me.

(I should point out here that this is true especially in the Northeast, where I live, and where a certain crankiness is the default position. In the Southeast, where some kinds of politeness, even if they are rigidly stratified by race and class, are much more common, my courtesy, when I am read as a man, isn't transgressive at all. In fact, it serves to reinforce that gender attribution. Absolutely nothing says Man, apparently, like fingering the brim of one's cowboy hat in a tipping gesture to a woman and her young daughter, saying first "Ma'am," and then, with a different smile, "Miss.")

This is especially true when that politeness crosses class and race lines. As unusual as it may be for me to address someone in a service industry position as Ma'am when I'm being seen as a transgressively gendered, female-bodied person, it seems to be even more of a shock to people when the midtwenties white boy I sometimes am does it. This may be the most gender-transgressive thing I ever get to do—perform the possibility that men can be courteous and friendly in a culture which allows, and in fact expects, its men to be rude and disconnected. So when I take the time to politely inquire how someone is feeling today, or comment sympathetically on a crying two-year-old being half-past naptime, or wait patiently for an elder to pet and admire my dog, I am having almost the reverse experience. These are things that the world expects from women (though I won't speculate here about why) and when I perform them it calls my masculinity and my motives into question immediately. If men don't do such things, why am I doing them? I become, quite against my will, an outlaw again.

Very occasionally, but most gratifyingly, it earns me a heady dose of approbation from a woman nearby. Part of that gratification is about being approved of, of course, but the rest comes from my sense of pleasure at having created or reinforced or expanded the possibility, in someone's world, that men can be engaged and attentive and kind. All too often I feel as though the heterosexual women in my world are settling for only a small fraction of what they want, because they believe that they cannot have anything else. Concurrently, I often see the heterosexual men in my life being only a small fraction of what they are, because they have internalized the message that they cannot *be* anything else. It's a great pleasure to imagine that while I'm out being the most politest tranny ever to step a booted foot in my local Dunkin' Donuts franchise, I may also be read as a place on the landscape of masculinity where a sturdy boy in jeans and boots can also hold a baby, both expertly and with joy (and the nice smiles from girls are a lovely bonus).

I enjoy it, either way. I enjoy having the chance to transgress in ways that are welcoming rather than alienating, and I enjoy the opportunities that learning from my parents' example has given me to maybe make some small slice of change. I enjoy knowing the names of my bank teller's three children and keeping rough track of the oldest girl's win/loss record (she's a three-season athlete who's also on a summer swim team). I like teasing my pharmacist about his taste in neckties and talking about singer-songwriters with my pharmacy tech. I like telling stories to children in airport waiting lounges and passing the time with the other poor souls consigned to waiting on a long line with me. It keeps me engaged and connected with my world and it with me, with my big fat genderfucking self, helpfully producing an extra pen and smiling kindly. Hi, I'm your friendly neighborhood outlaw. Welcome.

Getting Myself Home

I did not tell my parents the entire truth about this episode when it happened; in fact, I am pretty sure they're reading about it just now, for the first time (uh, hi, Mom and Dad). The truth is, I fudged the timeline slightly when I explained it to them. The truth is, the pain started hours before I got on the first plane, or even in the first car to get on the first plane. The truth is, I flew all the way home from Minnesota, including changing planes and a two-hour layover in Chicago, with that last gallbladder attack. Then drove myself back over the border, talked my way into Canada using my driver's license and a copy of my book as identification (I'd lost my passport, it eventually developed, in O'Hare while lying on some seats, writhing in pain), made it home from Buffalo, and went pretty much straight to the Emergency Room. Ishai met me there, because I was in so much pain by that point, so exhausted from twenty consecutive wakeful hours of excruciating pain, that the idea of being able to get help five minutes sooner seemed like a blessing.

Economically, this was stupid, or at least it seemed so at the time. My insurance covered nothing that happened outside the United States. I knew I would have to pay cash for whatever the Canadian doctors did to me, and by then I was pretty sure that Mister Gallbladder was having his swan song and was going to need to come out forthwith (I turned out to be right about that).

When I phoned them from the hospital, my parents expressed their worry and then immediately started asking how much it would cost, and if I thought I should come back to the US to have the surgery done. I explained to them that my surgeons, Dr Hoseini the incredibly personable resident and Dr Kim the extravagantly overworked surgeon on call, had advised against this. I repeated their worrisome comments about gangrene, necrosis, and rupture to my parents, reiterating that Dr Kim in particular, after having seen my ultrasound, seemed quite clear that it had to come out. Now.

All of this is true. I certainly didn't make any of it up, and I had my gallbladder out the next day on an emergency basis. But what is also true is that I could have stopped sooner, and had Ishai meet me in the emergency room in Buffalo, where my insurance would have been valid and I could have stopped driving a full hour sooner (and probably waited for my passport there too and never needed to talk my way back into Canada). The other true thing is that the miraculously nice doctors and nurses of Joseph Brant Memorial Hospital in Burlington, Ontario, were ready to sort me out so that I could have made the trip: pump me full of hydration fluids and painkillers, let me check out with an actively disastrous gallbladder, make a few calls, and have Ishai drive me back over the border so I could check into a hospital there. Buffalo has hospitals. Some of them, evidently, are of very high quality.

I did not mention that part to my parents, even though I guessed they'd feel better if I were being seen in a hospital in their country, one recognized by my insurance (though paying cash in Canada still ended up being cheaper than my US insurance co-pays—by a lot). I know for sure that my father suffers from a particular kind of healthcare-induced xenophobia and believes that all good hospitals are in Manhattan or Boston, with the possible exception of the Mayo Clinic and maybe UCLA.

Maybe. But a hospital in a whole other country? Where there was no one he could bully, intimidate, charm, bribe, or get a friend to call? Disastrous.

I knew all of this. I knew it, and even in my blinding world of pain I still flew and drove and got back home to Burlington where the nice people took my gallbladder out last Saturday night, because what I could not say to anyone until afterward, what I still feel tentative and shy about was this: I knew I would be safe in a Canadian hospital.

I am a masculine, mostly male-appearing person, with a female body. Even in a stylish turquoise hospital gown with none of my usual restrictive undergarments, I still look like every other big dude in a too-small hospital dress, sacrificing my dignity for medical care. And as any transperson will tell you, it rarely goes well when the medical personnel come into the room with your chart and lift up your stylish turquoise gown expecting to see one thing and find something else there instead. Most of the trans-people I know are deeply resistant to doctors and hospitals until there is no possible way to avoid them, because they know that where medicine and gender meet is not somewhere you generally want to hang around.

(And before you get saddled up going, "Well, I'm sure if you just *explained* everything it would all be *fine*," let me remind you that there are plenty of documented cases of transpeople being left to die by paramedics because no one would touch *it*. There are transpeople dead from being refused medical care because they had internal organs like ovaries and prostates that did not match their gendered presentation, and so on. Dead now, or got a lot closer than I care to. Some people are way more freaked out about gender than anyone who would read this book, even for school or for a friend or family member, can imagine.)

It takes a lot of energy to be charming, approachable, non-judgmental-but-also-firm enough to explain trans issues to people in a way that makes them feel somewhat okay with it. Frankly, given a choice, I'd rather not have to do that between bouts of vomiting. Which is not to say that Canada is uniformly a Promised Land of trans-acceptance. But my experience had been that, in general, most Canadians experience my Intro to Transmasculinity in much the same spirit as Dr Gupta, the ER doctor on the floor that day, did at the end of my little speech: "Well, that's not something you see every day."

She said this with a reassuring little smile, and then told me what was going to happen next (hello, x-rays) and afterwards proceeded to engage in a little linguistic dance where she avoided referring to me by a gendered pronoun even one more time for the next twenty hours. She arranged for me to be put into a room I would not have to share by bullying the psych people a little bit into giving up one of "their" solo rooms unless it was absolutely necessary. When she called up to the surgical floor for updates on my surgery schedule, she referred to me as a young person, a patient, and even as "the emergency gallbladder" in order to avoid having to call me a man or a woman, and I will tell you right now that as a transperson I have railed against being reduced to my body parts, and I felt a wash of incredible gratitude as I listened to her refer to me by my medical problem instead of by my name or legal sex.

I also know that some sort of off-camera briefing must have taken place, because the nurses started referring to me by pet names, instead of as Ma'am or Sir as they did with the other adult patients, calling me Chief, Sport, Buddy, and even Friend (as in, "How you feeling, Friend? You can have more painkillers if you need them") in much the same way as I heard them address the kids on the ward. Even the surgeons, who looked at me naked for some number of hours while they peeled my miserable gallbladder off my blameless liver, just called me Bear. The last thing I remember before my surgery was the anesthetist saying, from behind my head: "Okay, Bear, we're going to put this stuff in your I.V. now. You have a nice sleep, and we'll take good care of you." I probably would have started to cry from sheer relief if I had not, within seconds, been unconscious. The next thing I remember, when I woke up in the recovery room, was another nurse (a new one, to whom I had said tranny-nothing and had not given my now-standard hospital intro: "I'm Sharon Bergman, but everyone calls me Bear") bending over me, saying, "Hey there, Bear. Do you feel sick to your stomach at all?"

Even now, I tear up while recalling it. I feel relieved and grateful. As soon as I was feeling well enough, I bought boxes of fancy treats and handwrote thank-you notes and had them all delivered to the Emergency Department and the surgery. I also recognize that my gratitude and relief helped me in all phases of my stay there—wellness begets wellness, fear and shame do not.

I chose not to explain all this to my parents at the time, because I didn't trust that they would really *get* it, as considerate and caring as they are. They are personable and well-off and gender-normative and heterosexual and have great health insurance, and when either of them has had to go to the hospital it has always been under the direct care of a doctor who has known them for some years and is also well-respected by that hospital and in the field. They expect their medical experiences will be safe and respectful, and they always are. They've never had to go into a hospital with the reasonable expectation that the staff might hate what they are, fear their bodies, and feel disgust that they exist at all. That's not a knock on them; it is, merely, true.

The part I did not have to explain, that they knew to worry about all on their own, was how and whether someone would be able to advocate for me. They didn't quite know how to ask the question, but my husband won a million husband-points with my family when he understood my parents' frenzy to get in the car and drive all day to be there before I went into surgery without it being spelled out. He understood it as fear that, while I was unconscious, something might happen and no one would have legal standing to make decisions on my behalf (and earned a million husband-points from me by managing to make my parents feel understood and respected while still reassuring them that everything was, really, going just fine and so they could stay home). That one I can attribute squarely and securely to Canada. My marriage is legal here, and my husband gets all the rights that go with that without regard to his, my, or anyone's gender or perception of it thereof.

It is wonderful to have come out the other end of a potentially terrible experience feeling shaken but relieved. But in the retelling of this story what is clear is that I had a lot of luck and a lot of privilege on my side. I really should not have gotten on two different planes with my unstable gallbladder, since air travel and pressurized cabins are not so good for organs in distress, and traveled for fourteen hours. Also, I was fortunate as a professional trainer—explaining my body and identity to strangers is a particular skill set of mine. And even when I was sleeping or out of it, I happen to be married to another professional trainer who (and, in retrospect, *this* is what would have calmed my father down) is the LGBTQ health representative for our region and is also in charge of training the entire province's Human Rights Commission about trans issues.

I had every single possible thing on my side that a transperson could have—the money to pay for the care I needed, fluency in English, familiarity with medical language, plenty of experience and comfort advocating for myself, someone else to advocate for me on standby, a more-or-less trans-friendly country, and some credible legal threats if I needed them—and I was still afraid. I still flew and drove in excruciating pain to get to my place of most safety, and most privilege, before I let myself get any help. I was still tense and unhappy and nervous about every interaction for the entire first day, until it finally started to sink in that everyone was being really, really nice to me. I still know that the odds of a positive hospital experience were overwhelmingly against me, as a person of substantially non-normative gender. So when I sit still and let the gratitude for it all wash over me, it comes heavily flavored with how incredibly lucky I was and am.

The Rule of Two

The Rule of Two, if you ask any transperson, is a cruel joke. It refers to the difficult truth that one gender-variant person passes better than two, nearly always. One short, slightly cello-shaped dude with a wispy beard looks like just that, a minor anomaly of masculinity, but not far enough away from the standard deviation to cause comment, or even notice. Two of them, however, are a different story; ditto the two extra-tall girls with colorful scarves draped around their throats, ditto all the pairs and groups of genderfucking friends and lovers. One's safe, two less so (unless you can pass for siblings, which makes it sort of better), and three or more is asking for trouble.

It seems like a certain kind of meanness on the part of the universe that this is so. The experience of being trans is in some ways so unique—perhaps not in its emotional content, but in its mechanics and also in its fallout—that trannies band together for advice and reassurance and warmth and protection instinctively. I don't know the collective noun for a group of us, but whether we travel in a gaggle, a pride, a paddling, or even a murder, we do find our ways to one another, and this is where the trouble, regrettably, often starts. When we venture out with our kind, we are taking a certain maybe brave, maybe foolish, or maybe oblivious chance.

As a visibly queer, visibly genderfucking thing, I know this every time I leave my house. It informs my behavior, my dress and manner: Where am I going? Who will be there when I arrive to see me and read my gendered cues? Do I want to be read as queer or as straight? As a butch, a tranny, a cisgendered man (I can even do girl, but only for short stretches)? Who will I be with, and how attached is that person to hir gender, to being read a certain way in the world (because making the decision that I don't care what gender or sexuality I am on an afternoon is one thing, but I cannot decide that for anyone else)? What do I need to get done, and how will my gender performance affect that; do I need some gender in particular for it?

Some people dress for the weather, you know?

Some of these activities or needs are gendered themselves, like the trip to the hardware store or the interior design show-room, and some of them are just about who I have been before. The nice people who work at my dry cleaners all think of me as a very pleasant young man, and while I am not specifically invested in them thinking I'm a guy, I am also not in a great hurry to cause a big tranny kafuffle at my local outlet. I don't have the energy to be an activist all the time, and the dry cleaners is the sort of place I generally show up to by myself, no telltale trannies in tow to give me away.

These days, with great pleasure, I am keeping company with an outlaw like me, a sexy hybrid transman who lives in an un-modified body with great comfort and not a little style. You may chalk it up to love's hyperbole if you like, but to me it looks like that unshakable thing that Fred Astaire and Kurt Brown-ing and Mike Piazza all have in common; that loose-limbed, juke joint, hey-let's-go-again ease. It's a valuable thing in a transman; it suggests that any observer's sense of peculiarity is clearly all about that person. I fake it differently, all bulk and woof, a gen-eral pound-for-pound insistence on the space I'm taking up as I move but with the same general effect. While I'm alone anyhow. Separated, we're guys—he's a little more big-city faggot and I'm a little more *Homo ursus urbanus*—but no one bothers us about it.

> We wait thirty minutes for dinner on a Saturday night, crammed together with a dozen other hungry diners in a short and narrow hallway, hugging the walls to allow room for exiting customers to pass. He stands with his back to the wall and I, hand looped into his belt buckle, face the wall and turn my head toward him. It is an unambiguously intimate pose, shoulder to shoulder and facing. The other diners take notice, along with the wait staff. We hold hands all through dinner, feed each other avidly, and pour tea and sake into each other's cups with great attention. When we leave, the host shakes both our hands and urges us, warmly, to please come back soon.

Walking together on these early-summer evenings in Toronto, his city, holding hands as the light wanes and walking as close as two people in two skins can get, we break the Rule of Two. We're identified. We are both visibly queer, two homo boys with capricious facial hair and heavy steel earrings and an unmistakable interest in each other, and also, somehow, now visibly trans. There's something clearly off about the picture to the casual observer. We're a double threat or a double dose of familiarity, depending on who sees us. People watch us as we pass, gazes lingering a long time, trying to parse the sentences of our desire for one another.

Their conclusions are for the most part, obviously, about them; the eye brings what it sees to seeing. Apparently straight people try desperately to work out which of us might be a girl, sometimes assigning it to him because he's smaller, and sometimes to me because his unmistakable tidy goatee trumps. People who read us as lesbians, in general, give us the good queer nod when they think we're two butches but look bewildered and displeased when we're close enough for them to see how that might not quite get it, either. It's the fags who most usually acknowledge us as like items. By which I mean, like them. But also, we are like one another—whatever we are, we are obviously the same thing, *homo*sexual in the classic sense. Obviously, the same coordinate group, the same season, obviously the same gender, whatever the hell that might be. Two boys with breasts and beards, the kind of boys who queer a room just by entering it, and now, we're squared, in love, touching each other just less than what would be unseemly and leaving no doubt that we've explored the underlying topography and found the climate and elevation most satisfying.

> The coffee place around the corner is the closest espresso machine to our house-sitting gig. We haven't been sleeping enough and, while we can't fuck enough, we have certainly been trying our best. We stumble in unshowered, beg for iced espressos, flirt with the waitress who makes an extra trip for his soymilk and more or less invents two drinks to our specifications. She is charmed and friendly, all big grins and extra chocolate syrup at no charge. On the way out, I glance back, and she is watching us walk away, pressed together, and she is smiling.

And how do I dress myself to go out with him? In love, in a cloak of the stupid hopeful optimism of fresh love, which I imagine will protect me from both the wind and the weather like every other idiot in love has ever imagined. I hardly care what gender anyone wants or expects of me, or would like to see, or can; I hardly care what I have to get done in a day. I already know that anyone who sees us is making a mental checklist of gendered characteristics anyway, no matter what I wear or how I walk, and find in that the freedom to just brush my teeth and leave it at that. I'd rather look at him anyway, at his generous smile and long neck and faggoty glasses and really splendid ass. Anyone who needs to spend time looking at me can do it without me being complicit.

I sometimes say while teaching that gaybashing is usually about gender transgression, not sexual transgression; that people who get beat up for being queer are usually taking the heat for being visibly gender transgressive in ways that suggest queerness in the culture, that they are rarely committing acts of homosexual congress in the street. But we are. We are smooching and touching, making both our affection and our lust quite visible, and rather than drawing predators it seems to repel them, seems to create a bit of charmed space, as though somehow we're not quite the same kind of threat when we're wiping drops of soymilk off each other's upper lips, quietly telling stories with our fingers twined together, immersed in each other's voices. Has our society really come to a place of *amor vincit omnia*? Are we there yet?

I wonder. Part of me thinks the evidence speaks for itself; if two queer transmasculine things can smooch their way across Toronto and encounter perhaps the odd glance but also the regular encouragement and evident enjoyment of the people in their path, clearly something strong and fine is at work. Clearly, the tireless and honorable work of our elders and colleagues have made a kind of space for us in the world that they scarcely could have imagined and into which we spread out luxuriantly as formerly root-bound plants, repotted and revived. But part of me attributes this to a different kind of Rule of Two, this way in which this boy and I show our unapologetic queerness, our truthful inhabiting of our genders, as though there is nothing whatsoever wrong with us. It is maybe welcoming and maybe arresting, but it parts the seas for us. For me, when I'm with him.

If we're not hiding, if we're not fearful or ashamed, there must not be anything wrong with what we're doing. We can walk right out with our warm and vibrant and fresh love in our hands, or on our sleeves, and if anyone disapproves they keep it to themselves in public, like people who dislike chocolate or disapprove of recycling. We kiss and laugh, and look over each other's shoulders from time to time, but mostly right into each other's eyes.

In the kitchen of the house where we're staying, where all manner of people come and go at all hours, a fiftyish bike activist and peace protester named Jean is working on the homeowner's computer when we come downstairs one late morning, looking for bagels and coffee. We sort out the breakfast division of labor, and kiss, and when we look up Jean says in a deep voice, "Wow. You guys are just totally erasing the boundaries of gender." We grin, kiss again, and Jean makes us strong coffee to have with our bagels and fruit and love.

Like Love

I am holding the stack of forms for my immigration to Canada as my husband's legal spouse. We meet the requirements, but now we have to prove it: on paper, with photographs, with testimonial letters and bank documents and what-have-you. I'm more than willing, you understand—I am stupid in love with this boy—but a mounting number of places where the form doesn't have a useful option for us gives me a certain window into our relationship I don't usually consider. Like the part about observing religious holidays together. When my parents asked, "Did he have a bar mitzvah?" I replied: "Well, at that time it would have been a bat mitzvah, since he was a girl then, but no, he didn't, since he was Anglican then, too. He has been called to the Torah, of course, but when he was much older—he never got to have a bar mitzvah at thirteen with a big party like Jeffrey [my brother] did."

There was a long pause. "Oh," said my parents. "How interesting."

In the day-to-day, we're pretty much like every other pair of lovers. We've negotiated a compromise between his need for a vegetarian household and my love of meat. We rescue each other from potential lateness or overwhelm by doing an extra dog walk or the dry-cleaning pickup. I pack him out the door with lunch when I'm home from touring, and he packs me away for a week with love notes hidden in my dopp kit when I leave again. He always knows how to get where we're going and I never do; I always know what time it is and he never does. If you asked me to describe our relationship, these are the things I would tell you about. I'd say that we're good at communication and division of labor, challenged by how to deal with conflict. Excited to be thinking about parenting soon. Both self-employed and very happy about it. These are the sort of things I am getting ready to write on my maple-leaf-emblazoned set of forms, downloaded off the Internet in a state of excitement.

However, it is also true that I once had to give my parents a three-page set of terms and their definitions to help them understand me and my relationships and my life.

The other set of facts about my partnership, soon to be legalized by the Canadian government (knock on wood), is that I was born in New York a baby girl, raised in New England but with Manhattan bagels and sensibilities, and have lived my life being seen as a man much of the time for most of the last ten years. My self-employment is as a touring writer and solo performer, both on issues of gender, sexuality, and culture (which is how I say that I am a queer, Jewish tranny who would like to tell you more about that, but in language that my grandmothers could use at a Hadassah meeting). My parents still refer to me by my old first name and with feminine pronouns, even though I pretty much look like a Nice Jewish Boy, and if you imagine they'd find it embarrassing to use "she" to refer to someone who really looks like a "he" then you have clearly never met my relatives. Last spring, I went to Milwaukee to give a keynote address at a conference and fell in love with a Canadian boy who was born a baby girl in Toronto, who moved to England for a while and then back, and who holds dual citizenship in Canada and the UK, one under his gender-neutral name and one under his unmistakably female one. He was raised just outside of Toronto as a Girl Guide and alto in the Anglican youth choir, but converted to Judaism and is a Nice Jewish Boy now, too, who does policy and curriculum work around queer and trans inclusion in the public schools. For a living. His parents still call him by his gender-ambiguous childhood nickname, but he lives as a man and makes his living in part as what he calls a display-model transsexual.

There does not appear to be a space for most of this on the form.

Here's the best part—our parents have to write letters to say that, yes, we have been together for two years and, yes, they have met our partner, and yes, it really is a real relationship. I imagine the text:

> Dear Canadian Government,
>
> My daughter, who looks like my son and is Sharon on her passport but S. Bear Bergman on his bylines, has evidently fallen hopelessly in love with j wallace, whose documents apparently say that his name is Jessica Charlotte but whom we know as our queer daughter's gay husband. Yes, we agree that this is very weird, but last night we caught them bickering about who was supposed to have canceled the newspaper delivery, and we all know what that means.
>
> Yours sincerely,
> The Bergmans

At first blush, there isn't a space for a lot of things on these government forms. But as a traveling, tax-paying transperson, perhaps the most valuable lesson I have learned is that in North America, even if there is not a form for you in the general packet, they probably have one for you in the back somewhere. So I am optimistic that somehow, in the grand selection of forms and exemptions and ancillary letters, there is somewhere for me to write in all the details of this relationship, absolutely charmed for all that it may look a little strange. There must be. The Selective Service has a form called the Status Information Letter to exempt young men from the draft if they were born female (the Vice President of the United States, I learned while looking for the form number, is also categorically exempt). Someone at the IRS knows exactly how much of my travel expenses I am entitled to deduct as a self-employed performance artist (not, as you might imagine, a giant employment category), and if you look long enough, you'll find that you can use form 2106 and then take the total and add it to line twenty-four of the 1040 form with a special code to indicate that you're exempt from the two percent rule about miscellaneous expenses. The State of New York, if you ask at the DMV, will give you form MV-44, to which you staple an affidavit from a medical professional and proof of your name change, and they'll change the sex marker on your driver's license from M to F (or vice versa). Surely, there is a form for me.

And so with this peculiar, bureaucratic optimism I settle in. I write about how he picked me up in a hotel lobby in Wisconsin, and how I bought his parents hardcover books as Christmas presents, and I import into the text file on my computer the pictures we took at Christmas. (There's me, the big pink cheerful Jewboy, with his entire skinny pale British family in front of the tree. Wearing the paper crown from my first ever Christmas cracker, even.) I sort photos from our trip to Spain and Morocco, looking for the ones that show the most clearly "foreign" scenery with us also in them. I debate about telling the story of how we had a blowout fight on a street corner in Africa, right outside the post office in Fes, and how he almost stalked off and left me on the street corner, but didn't. On the one hand I don't want to write our blistering argument into the official governmental narrative of our relationship, but on the other I have rarely felt so in love as I did when I realized that he wasn't actually *gone*—he'd walked fifty feet away and was standing against a fence, glowering at me. And my heart leapt for the love of him. And, I'll tell you what: I have never been so glad to see anyone glower at me in my entire life.

All manner of things that contribute to the rich pastiche of love stories must pour through their office. Even being a one-transsexual-and-one-transgender-person couple (kind of like salt and pepper shakers—same, but different), even me with my driver's license that shows a different middle name than my passport and him with his UK passport that shows a different name than his Canadian one, and all of them with female sex markers. Even with my parents calling me by a different name than his parents use for me, and never mind my grandmothers, or my rabbi, or his, or any of the rest of it. Surely, this must be old news at the Canadian Embassy in Buffalo.

I have what is basically the equivalent of a scrapbook here, not quite up to Martha Stewart standards in that it is digital (and devoid of pressed flowers), but it serves the same function. In the front there's a narrative letter to explain how all of these testimonials, with all of these pronouns and names, actually reference the same two crazy kids who shacked up together on eight weeks' acquaintance because the weekend fling they had intended turned out not to be enough. And neither was the June we spent squatting in a friend's unused guest room, nor the rest of the summer when I swore I wasn't going to move in with him but couldn't manage to leave. That Sharon and Bear and j and Jessica and Ishai are all told only two people; two people in love.

From the outside, the questions are about gender and sex. You're a what, now? Can you get married? Will it be a same-sex marriage (I work hard to refrain from joking that I am hoping for a frequent-and-creative-sex marriage)? How will you get pregnant? What's the difference between a transsexual and a transgender person, exactly (and you're not alone, Dad, in finding that complicated)? And from the inside, we're trying to figure out how to ameliorate the always-late/always-lost gap and schedule our monthly queer Shabbos dinner around my touring schedule and his outdoor activity habit.

(I am the partner of a man who owns seven tents. I, a New York Jew whose previous idea of roughing it was the Holiday Inn, am prepared to live in the same domicile, in perpetuity, with seven tents. Take that, Canadian government.)

Which isn't to say, "Oh, we're just like everybody else." I am so tired of that assimilationist nonsense, and believe me, the cisgender couples I know, queer or straight, don't have to fight for an hour with a bank officer about if they really are who they say they are, since every piece of picture ID has a slightly different name. The straight people, especially, pretty much do not agonize about how to deal with the fertility clinic or whether it is safer to go through customs together or separately. There are plenty of differences.

But it is to say that love is pretty much like love. You have your song and your anniversary, your love tokens and your secret code words for things, your tender stories and your lustful ones. You spend all damn day trying to buy the first set of holiday gifts for your potential future in-laws. You fight and your fights become part of your love story; you're enriched by your disagreements and you treasure those too. You save your beloved the middle bite because he likes it best, and he saves you the end bite because you like it best, and what's more, you start to do this reflexively, even when you're apart, until one day you find yourself momentarily startled to have saved a bite for someone who is 2,000 miles away. You realize that you used to have two pairs of track pants, one blue and one gray, but that the blue ones are now his pair of your track pants and the gray ones are your pair, and you never even reach for the blue ones anymore, even if they somehow make it back to your closet. Tranny or not, queer or not, binational or not, whatever you've got going on, you could put together a scrapbook of love that would convince any Customs and Immigration officer that, however weird it looks, it looks like love.

It Only Takes a Minute, III

Two days after the wedding, I talk to my dad on the phone. He asks me how I refer to Ishai, now that we're married. I say that I call him my husband. And how, Dad wants to know, does he refer to me? It's clear in the question that he's really not imagining me as a "wife," but doesn't know any other married words. When I tell my father that Ishai also refers to me as his husband, there is a long pause and then he says, "I'm going to send you an email, with some questions." I assure him that this will be fine.

A guy on the street is wearing a black T-shirt emblazoned in hot pink with the words "I (heart) Breasts. . ." I turn, and see that the back reads ". . .but I hate breast cancer. Please, do your self-exam." I laugh and stop him, asking where he got the shirt and explaining that I want one too. He tells me and then says he's surprised I'd wear it. "Why?" I ask, expecting him to assign it to my being a gay man. "Well," he replies, "probably people will think you're a lesbian unless they read the back."

Four small boys are playing with chalk on a city sidewalk next to a hopscotch pattern. In a fit of whimsy, I hopscotch it as I go by. One of the boys says to the others: "Wow, did you see that? A grownup, and a *guy* grownup. That's like the weirdest thing *ever*."

I kiss my boyfriend at the baggage claim in the Pittsburgh airport. He's the first same-gender masculine person I've kissed in public, and I'm shocked at how much more staring there is now than there was when I was one of two dykes kissing. There's a wildfire of little comments across the concourse, and he says, "Be careful, please." I know on paper that people react to queer men much differently than they do to dykes, but this is the first time I have to worry about it. It's a little thrilling.

In a restaurant with my Nana, she hands me her purse before she goes into the restroom. I stand outside, holding it (large and pastel), waiting for her. Another guy is parked similarly, by his mother, and we start joking: "I don't know about that bag with those shoes," "Oh, it really brings out the color of your eyes." We're camping it up, mincing a little and laughing quite a bit, until I figure it out that I'm being misogynist and he's being homophobic. I shut up promptly.

Seahorse Papa

On the stoop of the fertility clinic, where we wait at 7:30 a.m. for the daily ultrasound, all of the women are very nice and exchange perplexed expressions only when they think we're not looking. What are you doing here? is the question their mouths are all full of but won't spit out. What are *you*—you two boys, you men, you non-uterus-havers, you fertility-unconcerned males—doing here, here together, here without benefit of a woman to explain your presence? The other men stand with their wives looking, in general, only at their female partners or their own hands, but we're an anomaly. There is no reason for a man to be here at this hour; this is the hour of fertility monitoring, of the motorized chair that lifts its sitter's ovaries to an ergonomic height, of the every-next-day visits for a solid month to determine when things happen in there. If things are happening at all in there.

The women on the stoop, being Canadian and therefore disinclined to do anything that may be perceived as impolite, do not ask. Not even when we go back into the ultrasound room do they say a word. Not when we arrive, sleepy and cheerful, and not when we leave holding hands.

And the staff say and do nothing to answer for it. No one stumbles and uses Ishai's former female name when calling him into the ultrasound room, not even once, no one "forgets" or slips up and calls him *she*. Not even once. I imagine that the waiting women must assume that there's some other reason for men to attend, some sort of new treatment or test they've never heard of. Maybe they imagine he's a sperm donor, or requires some other kind of ultrasound for some other purpose. I haven't asked.

Some of the technicians are quite nice, and some are clearly not on board with this program, but either way they're professional and efficient. The woman who opens the clinic at 7:30 promptly and takes everyone's blood is Gloria, whose boyfriend often walks in five minutes after she opens with a tall cup of black tea and a kiss for her, and she's our favorite among the staff, the one who refers to me as Ishai's "co-pilot" (a kind of gender-free language that we come to treasure) and has obviously seen and measured a lot of couples in her time at the gateway to baby having.

Gloria doesn't seem to care that we're trans and she clearly likes it that we're sweet on each other. I don't realize how much that affects her treatment of us until the day when I see her sniff dismissively at the back of a very well-dressed, polite white couple who are never at all tender with each other. I think about what it means to have your fertility phlebotomist's blessing or good wishes on the baby-making process, and I am glad to have it. Obviously, I am glad to have anyone's blessing, everyone's blessing, in this somewhat strange and yet also entirely commonplace endeavor, but it somehow seems especially useful, especially good and right, to feel that the woman who literally opens up the door for us to come in and begin this process would like for us to succeed.

Like many queers who are interested in parenting, we have discovered that heterosexuals are often curious about how, exactly, we plan to implement our small-person acquisition. It's the age of Oprah, so they've all heard about turkey-baster babies and adoptions from poorer nations and Indian surrogates, and it's not so much how as which one, with the options depending, of course, on whether they know we're trans or not. We've been so pleased with how our cheerfully matter-of-fact approach has worked at the fertility clinic that we've taken it on the road. "Oh, my future husband still has his uterus and ovaries, so we're going to try to get him pregnant." Any befuddled looks are helpfully clarified—"He's a transsexual, dear"—and, where necessary, the ways in which a female-to-male transsexual is different from a male-to-female transsexual more thoroughly explained (a tactic I was forced to adopt when I realized that my breezy delivery of the biological facts without a lot of explanation elsewise had left a couple of poor souls believing that male-to-female transsexuals could have reproductive organs installed, and use them to give birth. Oops).

But other than that, it turns out that the world is more or less composed of two types of people on this matter. There are those who do not believe that queers should be raising children at all, no matter who bears them or how any individual couple might come by them. These people hold the whole business as wrong, bad, and an abomination before their god. So the part about my tranny husband's childbearing plans, while perhaps the extra-ab-errant icing on an already-sinful cake, isn't really a big deal, and no amount of normalizing explanation about the mechanics of transguy pregnancy is going to do a damn bit of good.

The other kind of people, the ones who are fine with queers raising children, also do not care that much about the trans part, and that, I have to confess, is what I was not prepared for. When we made plans to start trying to get pregnant, I imagined fight-ing this battle on every possible front—going to war over and over again about our right to have a baby in this way, about the perceived and actual problems of gender, identity, body, and autonomy. I figured I'd have to make the point over and over that Ishai could be pregnant and still be a man and a father (or, in our case, an *abba*, Hebrew for father); that this was not an invitation for anyone to create hir own interpretations of his gender identity nor arrogate the right to judge it.

So far, not so much. Mostly there have been a lot of nods, some quite knowing, some clearly a bit befuddled and accompanied by a sort of questioning bob of the head, as people clearly hope more information will be forthcoming without them having to ask. But that's the whole of it, really; a lot of curiosity and hardly any hostility at all except from those people in the previously mentioned first group whose hostility walked into the conversation with them, spitting on the floor and muttering darkly under its breath. All of my well-practiced arguments, step-by-step explanations, charts, and graphs haven't seen the light of day once. Either I'm fighting a much more broad and basic battle, or there's no fight to have at all, just some explaining and then some reassurance that, yes, I do promise, I will let them know the very moment that the time to knit things has arrived.

I have no idea whether this will remain true as my beloved goes about preggers. I imagine that overalls and chef pants, the classic butch maternity wear, will also serve well as transsexual paternity wear, and perhaps we won't schedule any really dressy events just then. But because he's someone whose T-shirt slogans have often caused strangers to march over and demand he explain himself, I assume that his pregnant belly will, likewise, raise some conversation. I worry that the last couple of months (when he'll really show) will be demoralizing for him if anyone is mean or unkind, and upsetting for me (since I have been made to swear an oath that I will not pay a visit, carrying my big stick, to people who have been mean or unkind). I'm afraid it will stress the baby. I know already that I am going to have to police myself very carefully in order to mitigate my desire for Ishai and the baby to stay home and be safely unremarked upon except by me with regard to their utter fabulousness. Just in case someone says something mean. Just in case someone—G-d forbid—does something. I worry about that anyway, every time any of my beloved queer, freaky outlaws leaves the house, but my very own personal pregnant tranny husband bearing our child? Pass the Xanax, please.

What I am sure of is that we will spend a lot of time on the mommy conversation. Every pair of homo boys with a kid I have ever known has spent a certain amount of time discussing the apparently pressing question of "Where's your mommy?" In our case, the answer, "There is no mommy," is going to be, for a rare and delicious instance, entirely true. There is no mommy. We have a birth dad, a donor, and then me, which, on the one hand, might be more than I can explain in the supermarket, but on the other could be a pretty interesting thing to try.

Early in the process, I had a recurring dream about this that provided me with some comfort on the whole matter of making the explanation, and I continue to cling to it as my subconscious mind's very useful assistance in difficult situations. In the dream, a bossy woman in her early retirement years sees me out doing the grocery shopping with my (entirely theoretical at this stage) toddler son and, after engaging him in a spot of peek-a-boo, asks him where his mommy is.

"I don't have a mommy!" he replies, and when she insists in a somewhat patronizing tone that *everyone* has a mommy, dream me cuts in: "Actually, he doesn't have a mommy. He has an *abba* and a papa. And two great-grandmothers and five great-aunts and three great-uncles. Plus four grandparents, six uncles, eleven aunties, and a brace of cousins in varying degrees of consanguinity. Also a Tante Hanne and an Uncle Malcolm and an Ankle and a Spuncle and a Baba and a Big Pup—so really, it's probably just as well he doesn't have a mommy, as I frankly have no idea when we'd schedule time to see her."

And with that, in my dream, I wish her a good day and turn my cart full of spinach and cheeses and precious baby boy toward the next thing on our list.

I would say that. I would say all those things, and I would probably even be able to keep myself from going on a rant about what decade she thinks she's living in and how dare she give my son a complex. Probably. But I am not sure I would be able to resist telling her my favorite *Animal Planet* fact, which is that seahorses never know their mothers. They're borne by and out of their fathers, growing and being nourished and nurtured in the male seahorse's body until they're ready to be born, borne out of the distinctive curves of him. The father is the one who feeds and cares for the babies until they're ready to go out into the big ocean. I would say that we're seahorse papas, Ishai and I, not usual but certainly not unheard of among all the beings of the world, bearing our family into being between the two of us, out of our own distinctive curves.

Writing the Landscape

I do not think I am going to have as much time as I really need to write all the storybooks that my eventual, theoretical child will require. Even if I already had the experience and didn't have to learn the craft from scratch, I'm not sure I would have time. This is not ideal. Not that I am not glad about *Heather Has Two Mommies*, *And Tango Makes Three*, and so on. I'm simply not clear that the storybooks I am going to need are available yet.

Children like social stories, as I have learned while I've been thinking about, you know, making one. Social stories are the kind in which you read about or talk about something that is happening or, ideally, will happen to them. Seals go to the dentist, tiny blue aliens get tiny blue baby siblings, the parental units of hippopotami come to see that they have irreconcilable differences, mice fly on airplanes, and so on. This way, a child learns what to expect, and gets some useful vocabulary for thinking about or describing it. There are books for flower girls and dentist visits and first days of school and all manner of other things. This is very nice indeed.

I cannot, however, find the *My Two Tranny Dads* picture book. There are now two books that feature an uncle-daddy/sperm donor kind of character (including the oh-so-lyrically named *Let Me Explain: A Story about Donor Insemination*, which features, um, a straight couple), but I cannot seem to find much about our eventual child's relationship to our donor's parents, who are not step-grandparents of either kind (neither parents of steps nor remarried grands) but really-o, truly-o, naturally occurring grandparents of the kind you get when you have this kind of family. Also, I seem to have overlooked the bookshelf I need. Have you seen it? It'll be the one with the giant extended multi-ethnic queer family picture books, in which small persons are taken out to eat all manner of foods and participate in an endless variety of festivals and religious services, with all sorts of people in all kinds of places. You know, the ones in which ze learns to behave respectfully, by which I mean not yelling, "Why is that man wearing a dress!?" at an inappropriate moment. (Although, I'm guessing that won't be such an uncommon sight in our spawn's childhood. Ze'd probably be more likely to yell, "Smoke means fire! Smoke means fire! Get out and get help!")

I am not sure where I will find the *Yes, We're All Jewish, But Everyone Does It Differently Around Here* book for use when various players of hir small life observe Jewish rituals in an assortment of ways. Except, of course, because Ishai is a Jew by choice, there is one set of Anglican grandparents, so they are probably going to want to do Christmas things with him. I'm not especially concerned about this, because I have an idea that it will all be okay in a cultural-exchange kind of a way, as above: let us now enjoy the customs and traditions of our loved ones, which are not our own. On the other hand, I have seen tender, instructional books about Chanukah and Kwanzaa for that time of the year ,but not yet a "What's this Christmas thing all about?" book that isn't uncomfortably Jesus-y to me. So I think we're going to need that one, too.

What Does Daddy Do All Day? is probably also going to be a nonstarter, what with "diversity coordinator," "consultant," and "writer" not being the sort of job titles that make for books with fantastic illustrations. That, plus neither of us is going to be Daddy, I don't think. We do *know* some people who have verifiable occupations, though, which is good, and my wonderful brother Jeffrey works for an art gallery, so that'll provide a rock-solid field-trip opportunity to watch an adult at work and tell nice stories. Also, not for nothing, I read constantly as a child, whereas Jeffrey played a lot of video games, and many dire predictions were made about this. He's turned out spectacularly. So I hereby solemnly swear that if our eventual munchkin somehow turns out not to be a reader and has no special interest in all these many, many books, I will not totally panic. Feel free to remind me about this.

After small childhood, I think this lack of seeing hirself on the landscape might get easier. In books, I mean. There is actually already a decent book about a kid who gets bullied for having queer parents, and—

Did I just write that? What is the matter with me? I will tell you right now that I am having this unmanufactured emotion as I write, and further that I'm going to either sweet-talk or bully the copyeditor into leaving it in because, excuse me, but—what the holy fuck? Here I am rattling along about books I would like to write for my sweet little theoretical bundle of joy, and then I get to the later school years and go: "Well, that'll be easier, there are already books on being bullied because you or your folks are queer."

Disaster. Clearly, my work is just beginning. Especially because I might be starting to understand *why* these sorts of books are less widely available: in order to write them, an author has to feel ready to make a case about what's great, not just what's hard.

If you asked me right now, I could think of a hundred ways that having a large, queer extended family, including married dads plus a bonus spuncle (that's the fellow who donates the sperm, and no, I can't say it without snickering either) is great for a kid. So many opportunities, perspectives, routines, people to complain to, Chanukah gifts. There are stories to be told about how that works, both explicitly and in the byproduct-of-another-narrative sense. Also, I have a theory about kids who are raised in large, extended-family situations of whatever type and how they are more creative and adaptable than kids whose worlds are smaller and more routinized. And how about being able to find a mentor or activity partner no matter what weird-ass thing you want to try? Or having a bunch of adults who adore you and are not your parents to talk to about sex and drugs and introduce you to rock'n'roll (note to my family, both biological and logical: please observe verb/object pairings in the previous sentence). All of those seem as though they would make a young-adult book with room for the requisite angst and resolution, but also without it necessarily sounding so very weird as all that.

It's clear to me that being accustomed to a variety of kinds of table manners, that being a seasoned houseguest, that learning to roll with other people's food traditions and television rules will be a boon to a small person. I also think that getting to be a little fussed over and made to feel special on outings with people who don't have their own children might be very nice, especially if we ended up doing the whole thing all over again and have two of 'em. But I don't know exactly how to fit all of that into a YA book that is also, you know, about something (my general experience of the tween set being that a certain amount of plot is pretty much always required to carry them along). But regardless, it's not as though the field is crowded. I shall just have to try, and soon. I anticipate many revisions.

I heard an Australian writer on CBC radio the other day who had lived from age two until eleven in Sri Lanka (then Ceylon), and she spoke eloquently about her experience reading books as a child. Hardly any of them, she observed, mentioned monsoons, or desert, or other things with which her Sri Lankan childhood was marked. She spoke of a certain sense of being "off the world," somewhere not visible to writers or artists, and that this sometimes made her feel invisible, and at other times like a brave explorer. When the host, the marvelous Jian Ghomeshi, asked her whether she would have preferred her books to be more reflective of her environment, her answer was certainly instructive. Haltingly, she said, "Well, yes, in some ways, because I wouldn't have felt so . . . alone. But also, I had never . . . never seen a daffodil. Had no idea about them. So I knew from reading that the world was full of things I had yet to see."

I am not much worried that our eventual, theoretical child will read about heterosexual, cisgendered, closed parental sets and feel as though they are a wonder yet to be experienced or observed. Thank you, macroculture, for crossing off one of my Official Parental Worries. I'm pretty sure that's going to be a given in hir world. But I do worry about a kid feeling alone, in much the same way that other children I know from complex, queer families end up editing the details of their lives in order to sound more strictly normal. They report that they went shopping for shoes or to the rock gym with their uncle, quickly learning that if they use words full of cultural meaning, no one asks, they simply assume: your uncle, the brother of one of your parents. It does not occur to them that the uncle in question is in fact the long-time-but-now-ex-partner of your sperm donor, whom you liked far too much to separate from, and so regular dates are scheduled to see one another despite the fact that another of your cadre of uncles, the donor himself, would like to scratch his eyes out.

Perhaps I need to start there: a *Who Are the People in Your Family?* book, one that goes beyond a grandmother-as-caregiver book or a dad-*and*-step-dad one. Maybe a more fill-in-the-blanks kind of book, where young people can write the stories of their own families into the spaces. Or perhaps also a community-parenting kind of book, featuring baby marmosets (marmoset parenting is evidently a lot like human parenting in one key way: adults will bring food to babies who are not their own on a regular basis). In my book, a young marmoset will narrate about a series of people in hir life with whom ze undertakes a variety of pursuits—the mama marmoset, the mama marmoset's mama, the uncle marmoset who takes hir along stalking salamanders, the auntie marmoset who forages for frogs and brings them back as dinner, the other uncle marmoset who sometimes sleeps with the mama marmoset, and his twin sister who also lives there with all of them and is going to have some babies soon, making our protagonist marmoset a Big Sibling real soon now. And when the new baby marmosets come, everyone will get to take turns carrying them—mama and aunties and uncles and the brand-new Big Sibling, who will be careful and very gentle and very responsible. And all the other marmosets will be very proud.

Just a Phase

For the record, it's really as simple as this: I wanted to have sex. In some measure, I wanted to be having fond and tender sex; in other ways I craved rough and dirty sex. But at sixteen, like pretty much every sixteen-year-old in the history of puberty, I was prepared to take what I could get. Especially me, big and awkward as I was or at least felt at the time, I would take what I could get. And girls—girls were willing to have sex with me. They wanted to. Girls were smart and cute and smelled nice, so that seemed like a fine plan, and suddenly somehow I was a dyke and only dating girls, which certain people to whom I was related fervently hoped would turn out to be Just A Phase. And lo—they were right. The fact that I was living as a girl also turned out to be a phase, a turn of events that I don't imagine anyone was really expecting. But such is the way of wishes, I hear. It behooves a wisher to be very, very specific about what they wish for.

I like girls. I always have, and I appreciate femmes in particular for their many fabulous ways and particular skills, not the least of which is and has been making me feel like I am just 'zactly the right thing in a world that fairly regularly has taken time to tell me I'm a fuckup, a freak, or some other kind of disaster. Femmes, in addition to being savvy and sassy and generally elsewise charming, stood each of those accusations on its head for me. Through femme eyes, my masculine ways were desirable, my urges and impulses toward chivalry were admirable. My fear and shame about my fat and ungainly body, and my utter disinterest in revealing it to others, were re-imagined for me as the understandable reluctance of the stone butch to make myself vulnerable. To go with it, femmes attributed to me the admirable value of prioritizing the satisfaction of a woman. Considering that boys generally took the time to yell unpleasant things at me out of car windows and otherwise ignored me entirely, this seemed like a spectacular upgrade, and one for which I was very grateful.

But I never stopped liking boys. I came out, when I came out that first time, as bisexual. In the fullness of time I revised that to queer, because I had learned some new theories about sex and gender, and gained more understanding of my particular desires (as well as some new and frankly exciting things about acting them out). But it took me until I was in my mid-twenties to start thinking again about men, and sex, as something that might happen for me.

In part, this waffling and misdirection with regard to my sexuality was a failure of modeling. It was some time before I was grown enough to meet people who wore their complex sexualities in full array. Longer still, I think, until I was able to move through my hormone-driven, want-right-now phase and recognize what I was responding to in my sexual partners. I liked, and continue to like, queers and freaks and outlaws. I like transgressive genders and transgressive sexualities, especially in people whose expression of those things has a lot of whimsy, and when someone's sex and gender cues are all shook up I like that even better. As you might imagine, this is hard to articulate as a teenager (and was even more difficult twenty years ago, before the magical Internet swept in and normalized so many kinds of desire that had previously been served only by fervid imagination and limp mimeographed newsletters sent in plain wrappings). I like expressive, entitled sexuality; a cocktail of thoughtful gender expression and feminist sensibility. Show me someone who has examined cultural gender norms and cherry picked exactly which of those things suit hir and is serving them back with a certain style and a come-hither-or-fuck-off attitude, and I will show you someone with whom I could cheerfully pass at least a sweaty afternoon.

But there's this other issue, too. I like boys. Well. Really, what I like is masculinity, and what sort of genital or bodily topography it comes with is definitely of interest but not a limiting factor. There is a theory-enriched scholarly office in my brain patiently telling me that each and every one of the things I like about masculinity—sweat, fur, muscles, a certain fix-it attitude, authority, neckties—could also be embodied by the femininely gendered. This is true, and the femininely gendered people I have felt great desire for in my lifetime have all had, or been, at least some of those things in their own inimitable femme ways. But the more I allow myself to embody and enjoy my own natural masculinity— the more I move toward my most comfortable (if complicated) places of my own gender expression—the more I find myself interested in those (and other) traits in their masculine forms.

This has caused some issues, and not just because I am the author of a book entitled *Butch Is a Noun* in which I talk quite a lot about femmes. I don't really know how to explain what happened. I was never lying. I liked, and continue to like, girls— and especially femmes, for whom I have so very much esteem. I love the tender, brilliant dance of butch and femme, the ways that femmes have and do soothe some of my most tender places (and excite some of the others). Inexorably, though, the needle on the compass of my desires has been remagnetized, and now swings toward the bulk and woof of boys, even though so many other tastes remain the same: I still fall like a ton of bricks for the smartypantses, the storytellers, the activists. I still like bigger bodies, and remain fairly well convinced that there is no such thing as too much ass.

And yet, somehow, and with not a lot of warning, the more I moved toward masculinity, the more I wanted it. I know that I am not the only one this happens for, not the only masculinely gendered, female-bodied being who has suddenly been startled to discover, while buying cute boxer briefs, that ze was also lewdly imagining how some cute boy would look in them.

The adjustment hasn't been so difficult for me—I always liked boys, I could just never figure out how to go about that, as a putative lesbian. The fallout, however, has been substantial. The end of my first marriage eventually turned out to be, in part, because my fantastic femme wife no longer felt as though she wanted to be married to someone essentially living in so many ways as a faggot. While I have since remarried and adore my husband—and am reveling, even as I type this exact sentence, in fresh newlywed love with him squashed up against me on a plane—I regret that my ex-wife eventually felt devalued and unappreciated. A bitter harvest indeed for someone who did a great deal to redeem me from the nay-saying monsters in my own brain. It wasn't what I would have preferred.

And so now, I live mostly as a fag. I have fashion glasses and I put product in my hair and I am extra thoughtful about the housewares and I do unspeakable, delicious things with the other fellas when I get the chance (which is also complicated, since I am not in any way a Man, but luckily there are other queers who are queer for queers like me, and we manage pretty well together). I treasure the quantum femmes in my life who can still make me blush, can tune me up into my best butch behavior with a raise of the eyebrow or a certain, complicated smile—and I serve them as best I am able, somehow better because I feel fully seen by them. The husband and I, we have them over for brunch. I am always stirred to better locution, better manners, and better outfits by them—but not to heights of sexual desire, most of the time (there are a few lifetime exceptions to this rule).

And so it turns out that my mother and other relatives were right, and I was entirely wrong. Liking girls was just a phase I passed through. I indulged myself in it for a while, when it worked well for me, but once I was older my preferences naturally aligned themselves toward the company of men, and I eventually married a Nice Jewish Boy with whom to make babies. All of that, all those half-realized wishes made when someone thought I couldn't see or hear, turned out to be true.

Oddly, however, no one to whom I am related seems to be much placated by this change. I don't know why. It's exactly what they wanted.

Bowing to the Beams

Even by Bay Area standards, it probably looked a little odd. I was on my hands and knees on the concrete out behind the Ferry Building, cheek pressed against the ground, eyes scanning under the benches and beams lining the water. When I satisfied myself that nothing was glinting at me, I moved down a bit and looked again, ass in the air, clearly intent but getting increasingly frustrated that I couldn't find it. So when the nice straight ladies interrupted me to ask what I was doing, I couldn't resist a bit of snark and responded, "Bowing to the beams. It's a San Francisco thing."

"Um," they said. "Seriously?"

I stood up, brushed off my knees, and shook my head. I went ahead and explained that my boyfriend and I were playing a game in which we hid notes and gifts for each other all across the country as we criss-crossed it in travel. We'd leave or send one another detailed instructions, I said, showing her the rumpled postcard on which my instructions for this trip had been written. On the last item, I said, I was being thwarted: the thing I was looking for wasn't there.

"What about the others?" they asked with rising excitement, while their husbands shuffled their feet and looked uncomfortable.

Nodding, I said I'd found those: a slip of paper folded up and stuck under a table at the Bagdad Café, and another note at a coffee counter in the Mission. The first one had required peering under a lot of tables people were already sitting at, which caused some explaining as I'm sure you can imagine, but it's the

Castro, you know. I bungled the first attempt horribly, marching up to a two-top of transwomen and blurting, through the blinders of my excitement, "Can I look under your table?" I'm sure you can imagine how that went, but eventually I managed to explain what I was after and they thawed considerably, enough to let me peer under and see if my note was there. It wasn't, and in conversation it developed that they'd refinished all the floors in the two weeks' gap between Bobby hiding it and me finding it—a situation that gave me plenty of practice repeating the story for maximum charm value.

Number two was a quick grab in a nearly empty coffee shop with nice architectural details on the outside, but number three was looking grim indeed. He'd sent me to the same spot where I had sent him on his previous trip, a bench overlooking the water and also in proximity to a particular sign so it would be easy to locate. I was supposed to be finding a tiny metal box crammed into a crevasse under one of the beams at my feet, I explained to the nice straight ladies, but I couldn't find it.

By then, they were well into their Brokeback Moment, sighing happily over how romantic this was and exclaiming that no one had ever done anything so *charming* and *imaginative* and *downright magical* for them, all the while casting meaningful glances over their shoulders to their stolid, GORE-TEXed husbands, who looked a little cranky and a little bewildered. Gay men, they informed me with confidence, are just so much more *imaginative*. Then they announced their intention to help me find the tin, and set about peering under beams on their own while asking me a fusillade of questions: where did this boyfriend of mine live? When had I seen him last? When would I see him again? Was he my true love? Whose idea had the game been? Where else had we played it?

(The hapless husbands, it is worth mentioning, had fled into the safety of the building by this point, muttering something indistinct about more coffee after seeing their wives and me, like a mini-flock of nesting birds, scrabbling crabwise along on the ground looking for treasure. I hardly blamed them.)

At length, it became clear that we weren't going to find the tiny metal box, that someone else had almost certainly gotten to it first and snapped it up instead. I was disappointed, but not terribly—I had two of my three love notes, not to mention a great game to play and a marvelous boyfriend with whom to play it, plus I had gotten to tell the whole saptastic love story to two strangers who were just lapping it up. For a storyteller, that's a pretty excellent consolation prize.

The nice straight ladies, however, were undeterred. They questioned me further about the game, and when I mentioned that sometimes I'd had items delivered or hidden by out-of-town co-conspirators, they immediately volunteered to do that. I was agreeable, but when it turned out that they lived in Alberta (the US equivalent is roughly Oklahoma), I had to say with some regret that I didn't think it was going to work out. The game was played between cities that we both visited with some frequency, San Francisco and Chicago being the most popular sites, but I was hard put to imagine that both of us were going to have urgent business in Medicine Hat anytime soon. With that, they wished me good luck with the game and with the boyfriend and took themselves back off into the Ferry Building, clearly delighted to have had a Real Live San Francisco Experience with a Real

Live Homosexual. Very good stories for the folks back at home, this gay love story, helpfully delivered without anyone being subjected to the sight of actual homos actually kissing or anything scandalous like that.

But I got a story out of it, too. I tell it often, complete with gestures and voices and exaggerated faces (I'm told that my imitation of the husbands is pretty funny), to illustrate an experience of being seen uncomplicatedly as a queer man in the world, if only by tourists from Alberta. They were in love with the both of us, for a minute, in love with the idea of love, savoring the grand, transcontinental romance of these two boys, one of whom they were standing with, right there, in the weak morning sunshine out by the water, all of us still well-bundled in hoodies and coats.

To be honest, it's really quite lovely to have the story to tell. I have some stories of myself being approved of in various genders by people who want to flirt, and of people recognizing me in assorted genders but being displeased or disapproving, as well as story upon story of people either wanting to flirt or to disapprove mostly *because* they couldn't get a good, clear read on my gender. These two women from the Prairies, come to Sodom by the Bay for who knows what reason, found themselves a nice young faggot with a romantic story to approve of, become interested in, validate, and value. The weird part is that through them, somehow, so did I.

Gay Men, Queer Men, and Me

I am sitting deep in an old sofa, mostly dressed, with a naked man between my legs, his warm and furry back against my chest, his thighs draped over mine to spread his legs wide. We're on this sofa, and not in the warm embrace of his enormous leather-sheathed bed, because he wants to *see*. He wants to see my face while I have the use of him, wants to watch his own slick asshole gulp air and grin with wanting me inside him, and the huge mirror across from the sofa does the job perfectly. I agree because he's such a nice guy and such a hot fuck, but the visual both seduces and arraigns me: my body does not match this scene. I can enjoy pretending that his hard cock in my hands is really my own. I can tease his taint mercilessly, delightfully, never quite opening his hole with my fingertips no matter how many times I brush it, no matter how many times he hunches his hips up to encourage me. All the while I can forget that I have no balls of my own to slap and tease. But eventually, when his orgasms have finally sputtered out and the lights must, regrettably, be turned on, there I will be—sticky with lube and smelling of latex and poppers, cock in the sink. Unfortunate, unimaginable cunt underneath, all inward angles and slick wetness. I'll make a joke ("Hang on, time to swap out attachments") and escape to the bathroom and get all-the-way dressed, and tell myself this is all for his benefit.

Except for a few ill-advised and ultimately fruitless early-teenage fumblings, I never touched a man with any sexual intentions until I was one myself (or a near facsimile thereof). I have never had even the remotest interest in straight people of any sex or gender as sex partners; I like it queer. As a woman, as a dyke (or a near facsimile thereof), I attracted queer women—tough femmes with quicksilver grins and complicated lingerie and, later, equally tough butches with equally appealing, if simpler, undergarments. The queer thing was that I was called to other queers as like calls to like, as dragon knows dragon, and I reveled in an aesthetically queer sexuality (even when lesbo sexual mores or butch/femme cultural restrictions reared their limiting and limited heads).

But as I started to live more and more as a masculine thing, as my faggot sensibility began to crowd out my dyke history, I found myself increasingly attracted to men; to fur, to muscles, to the tang of testosterone sweat and its associated sexual hunger. Or, to be more precise: I had always been attracted to men, and I started to find myself willing to do something about that when it began to appear that I would be able to do it homo-style, the way that I preferred. Whether the man in question was the factory-direct or custom-built variety mattered far less to me than his masculinity did. My parts, whatever we were calling them, engorged at the right combination of skin and fur and ink, muscles and hard cocks standing out in varying degrees of relief; I had, and continue to have, delicious and nourishing sex and love with transmen, who are so willing to let my gender and my body be incongruent, who in fact enjoy my hybrid self. But—hesitantly and with a mouthful of apologies—I started moving into the community of gay XY men to see what I could see.

Gay XY men, generally, wanted nothing to do with me. While I didn't quite have to endure fish jokes, neither was I ever far from them. I cruised gay XY men using all the art and craft I had acquired from the bathhouse sluts who raised me from a wee small queer thing. They were . . . befuddled, and then, increasingly, hostile. How dare I know so much—the ancient and unwritten signals, the slight and intuitive movements of *Homo erectus*—and then turn out upon closer inspection to be a, well, not a man. The XY men who had been especially interested turned on me especially viciously; they would put the word out about my quare ways and in a moment both tag me with the stigma of pussy and shame any man who imagined he might not, necessarily, mind. *How dare I try pass myself off as a gay man?* seemed to be the insistent question. And I wasn't trying to, quite; I wasn't really not, either.

The problem is that I want to fuck men as a masculine thing but don't want to be a man; I want queer XY guys to be attracted to me in their queer, masculine ways and not see me as a woman even when the body I walk and fuck around in is unequivocally female. I want to eat my cake and have it, too. It's not at all fair, and I can hear the disapproving chorus in my head strike up a jaunty chorus of Pick a Side, Freakshow. The disapproving, however, may rest assured that I am not getting away scot-free with this gender crime (however often I do manage to, er, get off). In fact, I find myself inexorably hoisted on my own silicone petard, time after time.

I am aware that there are transmen, or men of transsexual experience, who have had no such difficulties. I am glad for them, and I am also entirely clear about the fact that I would have a far easier time fucking gay men if I embodied myself as a man; taking hormones, having chest surgery, something, anything. I did not, and still don't. I retain all of my original equipment in unmodified format. While dressed I look, walk, and talk like a man, even (I am told) fuck like a man, but naked, I am clearly not a man.

I talk a good game. Men who are starting to be seduced by my big body and big vocabulary—which is a small and particular kind of a group already—ask, bewildered, how I can fuck like a man if I was born female. I say that I have five sizes of cock from which they can have their pick and two perfectly good paws if none of those suit. I say that while I'm behind them and cramming their asses, they won't be able to tell I wasn't born a man and that if they can they're unlikely to care. Interested, they agree to dates, and I keep most of my clothes on and treat them to the kind of fuck I learned to dish out as a butch, the intuitive, thorough, masculine pounding that is wholly focused on the one getting fucked. I can, and cheerfully will, fuck for as long as they want and have no trouble about stopping when they're finished. I am not bothered by poz guys; though I always wrap my rubber rascal in a further layer of latex, there's no danger of it picking up anything unpleasant and no worries about it giving anyone anything, either. I make converts in my wake, alerting gay men to the pleasures of the transmasculine top and then make good my escape with my cock in my backpack and the bleach scent of cum still, sometimes, clinging to my clothes. It's satisfying and a lot of fun, and the sex is at least as good as the pleasure of turning gay men a little queerer. The post-coital hugs are always fond; often I am invited for a repeat performance on some future day. In that cheerful frame of mind, I leave before I can be exposed—and before I can get real.

I leave every encounter aroused, both hard and wet and full of longing, fleeing home for the comfort of my flannel sheets and trusty, gender-free hands. I am full of longing to be seen, touched, taken in as what I am in the fullness of my complicated body and extremely peculiar identity, to be met, and welcomed. To feel sure that my partner's interest isn't dependent on my scrupulous attention to eliminating any chance of unmasking would be a relief; the idea that a gay man might desire the body in which I live is almost unimaginable. And at the same time, this is safe: all of the demons and dangers of my anatomy—my fat, my unreliable body—are kept hidden in these encounters. I know that I am trading a kind of legitimacy for a kind of safety, in the exact way that I (and so many transmasculine things) have learned to frame a shirtless photo just exactly to the armpits. It isn't a true reflection, nor a whole one, but it is reassuring. To all parties.

I am as hopeful as I am afraid that one day, one of these tempting, handsome non-transmen is going to persist in trying to touch me; it's a fantasy as much as a nightmare. There's no part of me able to trust that this complicated body with all its speed bumps and dead ends will remain a viable route once someone is seriously considering setting off on it, when all the limitations are so visible.

I am painting myself into my own corner, every time. Telling an XY guy, "You'll never know the difference," means, always, making damn sure he doesn't. It means that taking off my jacket and hat is as much undressing as I can do. As much as I have enjoyed fucking a delicious naked person of any sex or gender while I'm dressed down to my boots, tie only slightly askew, this compulsory clothedness feels somehow different, as though without volition the experience turns on its axis to stonewall rather than welcome me. All the while, I think about what it would be like to take off the rest of my clothes. I wonder about how, or whether, that could happen. I imagine being curled up with an appealing

man in a dim room, the both of us sweaty and sleepy, having
been invited to sleep there and sort out the mess on the floor
in the morning. Skin against skin, roaming hands, and maybe
a long and promising kiss before the images flicker out, like the
end of the reel, a flapping nuisance in a square of white light. My
hindbrain, protective as ever of my tender heart, will not allow
this. It is clear (even if I am ambivalent) about how such evenings
must end, whether or not they actually take place in the evening.

We'll see. I'm young enough yet, and the world changes day
by day, and certainly in it there are the correct perverts to match
my particular desires if I am patient and make a space for them
to appear. They are probably not on *manhunt.net*, but that's all
right, as I may not be quite ready for them yet, either. Those
encounters and their cousins of genesis have their own pleasures,
and I am loath to relinquish them. I love the opening of bodies
as much as I love the opening of minds, and any opportunity I
have to climb inside someone and move things around a bit is as
rewarding as it has ever been, which is plenty. I will keep pushing
my greasy thumbs into assholes and laughing at exclamations of
surprise, keep recommending *The Leather Daddy and the Femme*
to my tricks, and keep making jokes at my own expense while I,
armed with my trusty array of Doc Johnson wonder wangs, initi-
ate yet another gay XY man into a queer place of desire where
people born girls don't always grow up to be women and sometimes end up sweet-talking bears with agreeably sized hands and
no compunctions about using them on you, buddy. And also . . .

Also, I will think about the next act, the one that happens
after the yelling and impact I'm so comfortable with, the act in
which Our Hero pulls hir head out of hir ass (and hir hands out

of everyone else's). The one that may or may not be possible but is nonetheless a possibility. To prove it, I have written an essay all about it. Maybe next time I'll skip promising him that he'll never know the difference. Maybe next time, I'll set about making *sure* he knows how the differences are at work. We'll see.

It's Always Easier If You Can Be Something They Recognize

My dear friend Malcolm is one of the kindest men I have ever had the good fortune to know, and also one of the more nontraditionally gendered (which, by the way, is saying something). I don't mean to suggest a secret eyeliner jones or a shoe fetish—most of the time, Malcolm's a Dockers kind of a guy, though he does occasionally rock a leather kilt. Nor am I saying he "wouldn't hurt a fly." He would, and to tell you the truth, if push came to shove, he'd be more use to you than I would, between his amazing ability to talk any topic into cowering submission and his lifetime of advanced martial arts training. No, what I mean is that Malcolm is almost entirely interior and almost entirely noncompetitive (unless you hand him the controls of a PlayStation), and that this pair of qualities, though it has otherwise contributed to a very excellent life, have made it hard for him at times to get jobs.

It shouldn't have. He's highly skilled at a software system whose expert architects are perennially in demand, and his work habits would make a nun blush and scuff her toe in the dust. But when he's set loose among all the other Dockers-clad software boys, something very particular happens: he's very clearly not their kind. No boasting or bragging or one-upmanship (or whatever the gender-neutral term for that is, though I suspect that this may be one case where the gendered word is the most appropriate), no competitive interrupting, no jockeying for position. None of the usual behaviors seen among the males of the North American Computer Programming Geek Elite. The result of this seems to be that the hiring people don't quite know what to make of him. I'm not even sure they understand what it is that makes them look at this guy—who aces the one-on-one phone interviews, who kills the practical test—and think, "Huh, does he really know as much as it seems like?"

I happened to be visiting him and his partner, who is one of my very dearest friends, a week or so after the last and most forehead-wrinkling occurrence of this. We're all genderphiles, and we all came quickly to the conclusion that something about Malcolm's innate Malcolmness was causing these HR people to rethink their decisions when he turned up in person. They could not, we theorized, map the talent, success, or skill they read and heard about onto the live-and-in-person Malcolm, who is the sort of guy you could be friends with for ten years and never have any idea that he knows how to rewire almost anything that has wires until something you owned blew a circuit. Something about his Malcolmness was killing the deal at the last minute. I had an idea.

"Next time," I said, "you should wear a band-collared shirt instead of a straight-collared shirt-with-tie, and display a dragon adornment somewhere on you as well. Don't get a haircut beforehand. Speak even a little more softly, and a little more slowly. Let them project whatever Orientalism they have onto you, and then they can understand you as some sort of Tao Master of the Database. Maybe you'll make more 'sense' to them that way." Malcolm is of mixed race, and was raised culturally within the Chinese side of his family, so I figured he could sell this.

We all laughed, but a little ruefully. "Can I bow?" he asked. His partner and I both nodded enthusiastically. "With your hands together," I chimed in, and then we spent the next minute or so darkly reeling off a series of Chinese racial stereotypes and evaluating which ones he might be able to embody, or even just invoke, to get their Chinese-chicken-salad-equivalent racial stereotyping working to his advantage. We thought, I suppose, that we might as well have a little fun with it.

Counting on racism as a way to interrupt gender policing. Whee. And now if you'll excuse me, I have to get to FedEx by five so I can put this paperwork in the mail to the Devil.

The truth is, there's nothing wrong with Malcolm as he is. One finds, however, that in the world of gender expectations it's much easier, and certainly more expedient, to change him to fit the cultural expectations of the back-slapping white yuppies of upper management than it is to educate them about the many and marvelous places of gender-nonconformity in the world (regardless of how very helpful that information could be for them). If Malcolm needs a job—and for the record he doesn't, just now, but if he did—well? What would you be willing to do to make sure you could house yourself, feed your family, walk safely through the world, or manage any other of the things on Maslow's hit parade?

Quite a bit, I bet. So would I. And this is one of the many places where all of the very careful explanations about transpeople's gender being the expression of their true selves is simply a giant lie.

It is quite a romantic lie, of course, which is our favorite kind, especially in North America. It conjures up tender images of young people crying themselves to sleep wishing they could just have a frock to wear, or elders on their porches grieving about what could have been (if they could just have had a frock to wear), and while these things certainly happen, they are never as un-complicated as the motion pictures make them out to be. If they were, I assure you, there would already be a Frocks for All Foundation, and well-meaning grown transpeople criss-crossing the country in a minivan, handing out gender-appropriate clothing to all comers. Particularly considering that many of us have lived some portion of our lives in queer communities and can therefore organize the hell out of a thing on zero notice, I am fairly sure this could be organized by no later than Tuesday before lunch. Even if we just collected everyone's old drag wear and pretransition leftovers. There would probably even be enough cash remaining to supply flowers to each customer.

While I love the idea, and while there have been moments in my life where I would have done nearly anything to be allowed to wear something that made me feel right in the world, it's also true that "making the outside match the inside" is only part of the story.

The rest of the story is about making the outside match something in the *Field Guide to Normal People* so that the folks where you live, work, or amuse yourself will recognize and accept you, allowing you to exist outside your own home without being constantly challenged. And that, it must be said, lacks some of the romance of the previous scenario. Malcolm's story, while darkly humorous if you tilt your head a little, isn't unique; there are many ways in which those people whose genders aren't in the first ten entries on the first results page have spent quite a lot of time either working to ameliorate the effects or learning to cope with the results.

Many things about gender have become so ubiquitous that

they're invisible until you fall over them, like curbs (which is a fairly good metaphor, since the verb "to curb" means *to check or restrain*). It's only when you sit up, rubbing your sore arm, that you notice them, that *he* notices how exceptionally rude a certain bank teller was, for example, on the day he turned up in his usual Saturday-morning fitted tee and half-worn eyeliner from the night before at the club, instead of his usual Thursday afternoon suit and tie. Or how much easier it is for *her* to get through her free-weights routine at the gym (including use of the Families locker room with its reassuring individual change rooms), when she's remembered to put earrings in and her hair in a girl-style ponytail. These are ways in which we serve, and even uphold, gender norms in order to get through the day, however much we might feel cuter or more comfortable in other clothes or makeup, however much we might enjoy a particular activity—or food.

(I can hear a dubious chorus cranking up in my mind, yelping, "Food? Give me a break. Food doesn't have a *gender*." No? By all means, then, see if you can get anyone you know who considers himself manly to go into a local restaurant where he is known to the other patrons, and among friends who know nothing of the experiment, and order that aforementioned Chinese chicken salad with light dressing on the side and a diet iced tea, one SPLENDA. Send me a photo of the expression of the waitperson's face, will you?)

So you learn to be something that is a compromise, somewhere between reasonably acceptable to you and minimally acceptable to the world around you.

To be clear: I don't mean this applies just to transfolk, but to everyone everywhere; it's just that transpeople end up having to do it all over again, and kinda quick. That makes it seem like a bigger deal. The more usual, cisgender process of gender policing tends to be a slow grind, not just in an overt boys-don't-cry/sit-like-a-lady way, but in an almost Darwinist way. Those of us who display behaviors that garner gendered ridicule or shame learn to erase or downplay them as a survival mechanism. To some degree this is a function of how much we natively care about what others think of us, and to some degree it is enforced by the people around us—even if a boy is perfectly happy to be the femmiest faggot that ever flamed. And even if his entire family is also perfectly delighted by this and cheerfully provides him with an endless stream of hair ribbons, the boys of the seventh grade are not always going to be on board. It doesn't matter if Young Master Femmetudinous is the best soccer player in his class, or grade, or school; they may well only ever see him as a pansy, and never choose him for their team. They will not credit him as what he deserves because they cannot understand him that way. Like Malcolm, his talents will be obscured by his gender presentation.

Unlike Malcolm, he doesn't (we hope) have to earn a living yet, so he's got some room. But if it is his heart's desire to play soccer, he is probably going to end up packing up his hair ribbons so he can play, or else dominating public-park pickup games forever, where no one can keep him from playing, ribbons streaming out behind him as he runs.

Perhaps you remember moments of this from your own childhood or young adulthood; some moment in which you ventured a thought or suggested an activity or wore a sweater and got a swift and terrible kick (metaphorical or actual) for your troubles. Maybe you noticed that being more soft-spoken made the boys like you more, or that being a bit less caring made the girls like you more (and yes, I watched the movie *Can't Buy Me Love* at least a hundred times as a teenager and thrilled at the protagonist's meteoric rise to popularity until he started treating the girls so unforgivably).

Whether we're twelve and wanting to be liked, or sixteen and wanting to get laid, or thirty and wanting to be employed (and also liked and also laid), we struggle to fit in. We struggle to arrange our gendered selves in ways that can be understood and valued by the groups of people whose company or employment or business or attraction we seek. For someone who has grown up and into the gender society who is prepared to accept and perhaps enjoy, the slow grind might be somewhat easier on the body, if not on the psyche or the pocketbook. Those giant industries devoted to helping women be more womanly and men be more manly? They exist to soothe, protect, or erase the wounded places where gender has ground against us especially hard.

Now, imagine doing it all in a year. In a year and as an adult, because, while school bullies and vicious parents and whoever else will fuck you up good and proper, that is something over which you can triumph if you can just get out of there through brains or talent or marriage or pure force of will. But when there is no out of there, and when everything is entirely pass/fail with no retakes, let us just say that the whole business looks a little different. However nicely I iron my dress, however tidily I apply my lipstick, however much I manage to grow and style my hair, I am never going to look like anything other than a junior varsity football initiation ritual on parade, and this is not a good corporate look. Or, really, a good anywhere look, unless you are on the fifty-yard line with a dozen other similarly suffering adolescents.

Perhaps more than anything, I feel resentful about this process and the lie it serves, and maybe not for the reason you'd expect. Of course, yes, I resent it because it damps or drains away our true selves, because it restricts free expression, because it forces falseness and creates pain, because it reduces the number of tutu-wearing soccer stars of any sex. Those things have an immediate and often negative long-term impact on people, even when they appear to solve short-term problems (like getting pummeled on the way home from school), by conditioning all of us to move toward safety, which by and large equals conformity. .

But my greater resentment is about the result, the normalizing result that makes me look like an idiot. I go about here, there, and everywhere talking (especially to cisgender people) about the many fabulous ways of gender. Insisting that gender is not binary, because I know that it is not, and that people of all genders can be successful in all things. I say this with great enthusiasm and a certain lyricism and many emphatic gestures, and people more or less almost believe me—until they go back outside and look around. At which point, they do not see the marvelous kinds of gender variance that I have described anywhere in their own lives. They conclude not only that I am full of shit, but more importantly that gender really is pretty much as simple as they had imagined. It is not.

But we cover up for safety, we become things that allow us to function when there aren't enough of us to disrupt the normalization process. So the exuberant variety of genders gets lost, gets erased, and no matter how much I or anyone insists that gender is not binary, it nonetheless typically shows up for most people as a binary. That reinforces the gender binary further, and then I see fabulous outlaws and shapeshifters and gender-resisters squeezing ourselves into that duality in order to work or play or just get through the afternoon. And I am sure that this is not the way this was supposed to work. Right? Talking about gender variance and coming out as trans and saying Fie on Gender Normativity a lot of times was supposed to make room for *more* gender fabulosity.

One bright pansy popping through a sidewalk crack will get weeded or stepped on; it's not until twenty fabulous flowers bust through and the pavement is ruined anyway that someone decides maybe it isn't a sidewalk at all, but a flower garden.

So please, for the love of gender—go bloom. Or water someone else while they do. Meanwhile, I will be shopping for a bright pink shirt and a luxuriantly flowered tie for Malcolm to wear with his leather kilt to his next job interview, whenever that is.

Shame

The wonderful writer Nancy Mairs, a woman with multiple sclerosis who has written several books about her life which include her experiences with the disease, perfectly describes the differences between embarrassment, guilt, and shame in her essay "Carnal Acts." Embarrassment, she writes, is what you feel because of what you do, acting stupidly or awkwardly, and guilt is what you feel because of what you should have done and didn't do, or did and shouldn't have done. But shame, Mairs writes, is the most poisonous; it is what you feel because of what you *are*.

Though I had never managed to articulate the distinction as well as Mairs has, I have organized my life as though I understood it that well. I imagine shame as a dark and subterranean thing, slimy and cool and lurking, curling itself around our lives and then beginning to rot and smell. The inevitable serpent images come to mind, but a snake is a far kinder and more pleasant thing than the item I envision. That sort of sightless, hungry worm that lives in the unfortunate sludge at the bottom of a trash can in the garage is more what I mean; the foul thing that even the most softhearted person who carries potato bugs out of the house between a drinking glass and a magazine subscription card doesn't mind bleaching into oblivion. That's the thing I mean. And when they are in our trash cans, we do it righteously. A good scrub, a few days out in the sun, and the slimy, stinky thing is a dim memory. No more unpleasant smell, decay under control, the whole arrangement working nicely again.

I have an idea that the decay is caused in the shady sides of our tender hearts by the same things that tend to cause decay in the natural world. Sometimes it's the untended wound that is ignored rather than being dried and dressed and protected: whether the quick slice of being cut out of one's family life for being queer or trans, or the long miserable abrasion of disapproval, of displeasure, of distaste. We have so many things to feel shame about, some days it feels difficult to know where to begin.

We are made ashamed of who and how we love, and in what ways this sets us apart from the mainstream. The bitter truth is that even when we grow up and live in our own self-actualized lives there is often still this particular place of decay that we can never address. We tell ourselves we're past it, but we do not look at it too much because looking too carefully comes with being smacked all over again with how our parents or grandparents made a much bigger deal about our heterosexual siblings' weddings, or how we sometimes just do not come out to cabdrivers or postal clerks. Or how the weirdness of never dating in high school when everyone's a clueless thirteen-year-old fumbling around trying to figure out sex pushed us toward bad choices when we started dating so very, very long after we wanted to be having sex. (Or what we did to experiment with sex when there were no appropriate dating options; perhaps you were better about this than me, but I was only barely smart and self-protective enough to stay clear of the Very Bad.)

We feel shame about our bodies, what they want, how they look, and for transfolks it not just how much they don't look like a magazine cover, but how they don't look like anyone we would want to be, ever. We both do and do not want to look at them, and we examine ourselves for any hint of the gender or sex we want for people to see when we're out in the world. We are told we're freaks, and not in the nice way that I mean it when I say it, either. We can replay the crash of being mispronouned by one person for weeks, or months, the feeling of the body like a whole shelf of glass and china crashing unchecked to the ground—noisy, dangerous, unmendable. And G-d forbid we should ever want those bodies, these complicated trans bodies, to be touched by another person. The shame of this begins with the fact that the common vernacular does not even have words for us, for what we have to be touched or how we want to touch, fuck, love, revel in our or others' trans bodies.

We have no words for the kinds of families we create, no way to talk about how all of these things have happened to us, no sense that we are not alone or, at least, in community at the sufferance of a few people who we believe are somehow far better or smarter or more "real" than we are, who have read all the right books and know the Official Trans Answers. A community from which we could get booted at any moment, without warning, if we cannot make ourselves sufficiently likable.

So these wounds fester. We cannot reach them ourselves most of the time, and we often do not even know what to tell someone we believe might be willing to help us, if we could stand it. Sometimes it's okay if we tell another trans or gender-adjacent person, but mostly it's like asking the pharmacist for medicine to heal a part of the body she's never heard of. And like a wound to the body, whether it heals even while you pretend it doesn't exist or gets worse and worse, depends in some part on your overall well-being. Depends on the shame load you're already carrying. Depends on how well you are able to tend the other areas of your health.

In a culture and time that offers us a never-ending series of messages about how we're bad, wrong, and different, it's easy to get overwhelmed by them. Easy to let things slide, easy to skip what we know is good for us, easy to turn to cheap fixes with big highs and bigger lows, but while we're busy distracting ourselves by poking our pleasure centers with a stick, those injured places don't heal. They get worse. They become the portals through which other damaging ideas enter when the tough and flexible skin of our psyches is too badly damaged to keep them out. We've all felt this, though I hope for your sake it's been a while; I hope that by the time you're holding this you've been able to get clean and dry and dressed and treated nicely somewhere they like you and want you to be happy (almost as much as I hope that you remember how extraordinary that is, and make sure to offer it to others as soon as you have your strength up).

Then there is the other decay, the specific one, the kind of shame that is planted and grown and encouraged, and I wish I did not have to write about this kind. I wish it, but I've been there and so have a whole lot of the transthings I adore, and if we are going to stop this, someone is going to have to talk about it. That shame is the repeated freeze-and-thaw cycle; love and being shut out and then redeemed again, over and over. We get into the clutches of someone who feeds on our shame, all the shames enumerated above, who tells us that we are too freakish or fucked-up to be loved, that no one else would ever want us. They sell us on the idea that however badly they want to mistreat us, as least we're not alone like we deserve. They freeze us out and then heat us up again and, baby, the end of this movie does not *ever* feature the asshole holding the end of the string realizing in a flash what many wonders and pleasures the sweet freak has to offer the world. I am sorry to say it, because I know in my bones that some people reading this are in that place this minute, and still hoping they can, in fact, live on a diet of shame and recrimination forever if it features very occasional fat juicy steaks (tofu, beef, or otherwise).

Maybe you can. But it is not a good idea. When you eventually get free of this toxic bullshit, you will find that every unexamined area has developed the sickening aroma of shame in the exact same way that food frozen and thawed too many times will spoil fast but never rot away; it will just hang on and hang on, tricking you with the idea that it is still viable. It is not. What you need to do is chuck it out right away. And if the person who has helped you to create it needs to go as well, in order to make sure that you don't spend your life throwing bits of yourself off the back of the sleigh involuntarily, then send them out with all the wrapped and reeking packages of your shame in their arms. I swear, I absolutely promise that if you can, there will be better things ahead. That thing about how no one else will ever love you is almost certainly not true.

And if you can't get free—if you're really sure that ze'd kill you if you tried and you can't see any way out right now—then please stay alive. However you have to. Please scheme and save and plot; please have a secret email address you access only from the library with which you reach out for help; please remember that you are precious and that living to fight again another day is a lot.

I am full of advice, of course (anyone who has ever met me for even five minutes isn't surprised at this), but I am shitty at this particular follow-through. I have not yet managed to evict my shame, or expose it to the healing elements until it curls up and dies. In fact, what I notice in myself is that I protect and defend those chilly and dim places of my soul, sometimes far more vigorously than I am able to care for the well-lit spots. I keep other people, even those whom I perceive to be armed with bleach solution and sunlamps for the shameful heart, far away. Maybe especially them, because there's a further truth to shame for me, and I think for many of us, which is what keeps us from ever opening up those places so they can heal. I am ashamed of them. And ashamed to be ashamed of them in a cycle of nested unpleasantness that leads me to package the entire mess in heavy black psychic plastic, stash it under the concrete back steps of my body, and pretend it doesn't exist. I do not want it, but I also do not want anyone to know I have it, and the exposure to air and sunlight necessary for dealing with it means, among other things, that other people might see. So when anyone, no matter how well-meaning, gets close to it, I say, "Look! A bird!" (or the conversational equivalent) and change the subject. No, thank you. Lots of thank you, actually, but a substantially larger amount of No.

I cannot seem to protect my pleasures or warm places by hiding my shame, though. When someone bent on causing damage to me wants to trash a warm oasis of joy in my life I can almost never stop them. I wish I could; I wish for the equilibrium to smile as gently and politely as I do at the person who wants to help and ask them to please, very kindly, fuck right off (which seems to work just *fine* then!). But somehow, this is not possible, and I am beginning to trace the reasons for this to the increasingly foul miasma around the back stairs. That shame, which I have allowed to sit and stew, begins to affect the rest of me as surely as a rotten piece of food makes every other item in a re-frigerator taste terrible. Over time, I and you and all of us begin to believe that all of us is as horrible as the parts we are ashamed of. They all smell and taste the same.

I am feeling brave at my keyboard; I want to make a laundry list of what I am ashamed of right now and publish it in this book and let everyone in the world see the Superfund sites of my internal landscape, with latitude and longitude and an open invitation to do-gooders of all varieties to come and bring their rubber gloves and bleach. In this moment, all alone in my office except for the dog, I feel as though I could almost allow it. As though there were some way in which I could start to heal myself.

Instead, I try to heal other people, which I trick myself into thinking is both Better and More Noble, when, in fact, it is largely impossible and basically useless except as a good way to keep me distracted from my own shames. Knowing this doesn't stop me, of course. It turns out that it's hard to encourage someone to let go of hir shame when you're actively protecting yours; oddly, they don't seem to really invest in what you're saying. It is from this that I came to understand the shame-as-a-rotten-thing-in-the-fridge effect. In whatever unknowable way, it's not just me who can smell it. Some role model.

As a storyteller, I strive to fulfill that tradition's ancient function, to transmit the values of the culture in which I am raised. But also, like a lot of storytellers, I have the opportunity to slip in a bit here and there about what I would prefer those values to be, or at least the direction in which I would like to see them move. Many of the modern storytellers I know, whether in theater or writing, write into their work the messages they wish to sell.

When I locate sites of shame in myself and display or perform them, it not only heals me, but (I dearly hope) it acts prophylactically against other shames for other people; opening the curtains or luring it into the daylight in the kinder metaphors, turning on the heat lamps and dragging it into the burning sun in those a little less nice. I have started to write not only about shame but also to it, or maybe against it; have started to talk about my refusal of the pity narrative as much for my own benefit as for anyone else's. Please notice here that I am more or less tricking myself into doing my own work. I package it up for the suspicious peering protection department in my own brain as something to help other people, and in the process break my own fucked-up shames wide open, one at a time. I am as ever a proponent of doing whatever is needful to take care of yourself, by which I almost always mean you—you should take care of yourself—but occasionally I manage to do it myself, and if you have to do an end run around your hindbrain in order to take care of yourself sometimes, just remember that it still works, no matter how you get there. Necessity is the birth parent of invention.

But here is the other thing I have learned: when I say that something is a source of shame for me, it opens something between me and everyone else who feels that shame. When I talk about how the constant stares and glares and whispers, challenges and upsets, homophobic ads and gender-policing television shows, really pile up on me and grind me down, or how past lovers (and not that long ago, either) have worked me down to a smear with their freezes and their thaws, it makes a way. Sometimes it makes a way better than the praise-singing I do in my work to counteract the shame messages. Sometimes the redolent and diseased places of shame, when I can inhabit them with someone else, are such disaster sites that they inspire disaster behaviors of the good kind: everyone bands together and shares resources. And as much as I resist being part of a group of people bound in part by shame, maybe I and we and all of us have to accept it before we can transcend it.

Perhaps it will require all of these things to help us, to heal us. Maybe all these shames *and* all of these new messages *and* all of our good intentions and sunlight and fresh air and all the rest of it are what we'll need to walk forward without any shame at all. To eliminate even the last lingering fruity trace of decay. To be the people that I and we and you and all of us would like to be— real role models, so that we can one day imagine a generation not hobbled by shame, not distracted constantly from the valuable work we need to do by the damage done to us, but ready to live entirely in the light.

It Only Takes a Minute, IV

I like going to the gym, but the locker room situation is troubling. The men's locker room is all open spaces and gang showers, and I know better than to try strolling into a women's locker room these days. It keeps me from going to the gym for months, until we move and change YMCA locations; the new one has a Family Locker Room with one curtained stall and one private shower. This seems like salvation until I notice that no one can parse why I am using it without kids in tow; my presence reads as creepy.

After readings of *Butch Is a Noun*, femmes often ask, quietly, if I'm on testosterone or if I'm "still a butch." For a while I declined to answer, because it felt like a very private question from a stranger. Now I decline because I reject the premise of the question. Even if the border were really that well-defined, border crossing is rather a queer specialty, ain't it? When I remind them that butch archetype Leslie Feinberg took testosterone, they insist, "But not anymore," as though they know for sure and then, much more tentatively: "Right?" Honey, I wouldn't tell you if I knew.

In the run-up to the wedding, someone asks me if I'm worried or anxious about all the facets of my life, all those names and pronouns, all in the same room at the same time. I hadn't been, but suddenly I am. Later, I joke with my brother that we'll make up a Pronoun Bingo card to encourage guests, by strategic mingling, to meet someone who uses each of the possible name-and-pronoun combinations for me.

When people ask me how my art is influenced by my gender, I want to say: if I had a flat chest, I would carry a bag. Or if I liked having my tits visible. A messenger style bag, maybe, or a backpack. If I carried a bag, I could stock it with my camera and sharpies and chalk and homemade stencils and some spray paint. A little dapping hammer, maybe, and some finish nails, and I'd carry little treasures I could tack to a doorway or wall. Or some flower bulbs, or seed bombs for turning median strips into tomato gardens with not-quite-volunteer tomatoes. Voluntold tomatoes. But. Since I don't, I don't, and that means I don't.

The indignity of your mid-thirties is that your joints and so on don't do what they used to, especially if you spent a good deal of your twenties lifting poorly and lugging too many boxes up the stairs in tacit competition with the other helpers. Last time I helped schlep someone's stuff I was hurting already, and asked if I could hold doors and carry lighter items. Someone said to me in response—I decided, later, trying to be funny—"No more wife, no more moving. Was the rest of the book a lie, too?"

Sing If You're Glad to Be Trans

Delivered on Trans Day of Remembrance, 2008, at the University of Chicago LGBTQ Resource Center

Thanks very much for having me here today.

I guess it makes sense that if you're going to have a really great-looking audience, it would be during a trans event at one of the most trans-friendly colleges in the country, right? I mean, we're not even going to talk about how long I spent picking out shirt, tie, and cufflinks for this speech. Normally, I'm with the students in Abnormal Psych 101 at eight a.m. Not exactly a big challenge to out dress the audience—I've bathed. I win.

I'm making jokes because I'm a little nervous. I'm nervous because I feel like I am about to say something that I'm afraid some people are going to be very cranky with me about, and I don't want to upset people. Well, I do—I just don't want to upset people I like. You know what? Never mind. I'm ready now.

I tried to write a nice, balanced, logical speech. I sat down three mornings in a row with my espresso—actually, that makes me sound butcher than I am, what I actually had was a double iced soy mocha, because I really prefer my coffee drinks to be as gay as possible. But I sat down with my coffee and laptop and I tried to Write a Speech. And it ended up sounding exactly like that—plodding, lugubrious, like something you do on a Sunday, wearing your scratchy good clothes with your Aunt Petunia. Like the speechifying equivalent of seventeen-grain bread: good for you, but not really a pleasure.

And why am I afraid people might be angry with what I'm going to say? Because I am going to talk about all the ways it is great to be trans, and some people are not ready for that yet. There have been some gains made in some people's lives, with a narrative of difficulty, of pity, of shame and eventual overcoming of shame into, perhaps, a grudging acceptance. Me? I'm in it for pride. I think that pride serves us better as a movement. Look at every other successful, or evolvingly successful, civil rights movement—they have all been about pride. All been about naming, claiming, and celebrating the things that make us special and different. They have all been about putting on our cutest clothes and being out in public, being counted. But I also think that pride serves us better as individuals. How healthy is it to rehearse our hard stories, our shames? How healthy is it to become part of a community best known for being raped and killed on the news and in the movies, a community with a legacy of fear, of keeping silent because the culture cannot handle us. Some people, for an infinite number of very valid reasons, need to keep silent. They have terrible, proven reasons to hide. They value their survival, and they should, and if you need to remain stealthy to survive, then do it, because we need each and every transperson alive. But I don't have to remain quiet, and so I will not talk about transpeople in any other way but as fabulous creatures of great and many wonders who are not, in fact, just like you. And I will not stop insisting that this is a good thing. That "just like you" is a phrase we do not need; we can be fully human and fully present and real and fully able to empathize and be empathized with. We can celebrate our commonalities without being the people of the "just like you." We can revel in our unique excellent qualities, and we can take pride in them.

And I want to offer some pride. I want to offer some pleasure. We need some, queers and trans things, in this day and age, and what's more we need some that is made out of real queer and tranny goodness and packaged by homo hands and served up to us, not created out of Hollywood and sent via the marketing department. We need transpeople to stand up and talk about when things are good, too—when they are great. I am frankly tired of showing up for trans events and listening to people talk about nothing but how hard it is to be trans. I am tired of being invited to come and Tell My Story, when I know that what the nice, well-meaning white lady on the other end of the phone means is "come and make yourself an object of pity, reveal all your secret hurts, and let us use them to find you blameless in your condition and therefore have sympathy for you, and give you some rights. Well, maybe not rights. But help. Well, maybe not help. But we'll stop acting like you're the bad kind of crazy and start acting like you're the sad kind of crazy. Is that better?"

No. No, thank you, it is not any damn better.

Julia Serano has a new book out, called *Whipping Girl*, in which she talks about the two dominant trans narratives, the pathetic transsexual and the deceptive transsexual. This is not enough for me. You don't look pathetic. Do you feel pathetic? No. And I am not deceptive. I hardly even cheat on my taxes and, baby, that is more than a lot of straight people can say. The fact that I am not revealing a constant loop about what, exactly, is in my pants isn't deceptive—it's a little thing I like to call having boundaries. You with me, here? I thought so.

So I'm not going to Tell My Story in the great tradition of the pity narrative. How can that be good for us? I mean, there's pretty solid research to show that houseplants wilt if you speak negatively to them all the time and thrive if you compliment them. Houseplants. I am not a botanist, but I am pretty sure that beings with brains and spines and, you know, feelings might also be affected by endless negativity. Might also wither, might also grow stunted, might also be prevented from the great blooming of which we are capable when all we ever get to hear are the endless repetitions of bad, shameful, wrong, and bad some more. So no more of that for me.

I want to talk about what's great about being trans. This is not to say that nothing about it is hard. I've had hard times—we all have. We've all struggled. We've all second-, and third-, and eighth-guessed ourselves and then finally come at great cost to a place of feeling confident in our identities only to have other people start the interrogation all over again. We've all fought with our loved ones, we've all waded through a mountain of paperwork that never does what it's supposed to do, we've all felt unsafe, we've all felt out of place, we've all felt confused and frightened, we've all been felt up by airport security at seven in the morning. Been there. We've all handled misunderstandings and mispronouns and mistakes; we've all been laughed at, we've all been asked who we think we are.

Who we think we are. People say that like an accusation, like it was a surefire way to make us cringe. It's a middle-school bully accusation, even when the bullies are the teachers or the principal, and I think we all know how that goes—someone looks at you and says, sneeringly, "Who do you think you are?" But I'll tell you, we know who we think we are.

That's the first great thing about transfolk—we have thought about who we are. We've thought about it a lot. We have thought about our genders and our bodies, but also we have had a lot of other things to think about, haven't we? We examine every action, attitude, gesture, choice of work or hobby. We think about what drink we order in a bar and we think about how we wrap our scarves around our necks, for sure, but we also think about how we want to be in the world. We don't follow a path, we forge our own. We have to. And it makes us thoughtful. It makes us all recognize that we do have a choice about most things, that we can define and enact who we think we are.

This is valuable beyond measure. Most people grow up fitting more or less well into the ways their families of origin think about things and do things. There is a way to do things—set the table, dress for church, study at college, conduct relationships— that is the Right Way because it is the way that their parents and grandparents and so on have done it. There's no need to question the rightness of it. But what transpires with transfolk, as we grow into ourselves and realize that we are not going to follow through the door into manhood or womanhood that someone is holding open for us? We also start to understand that a lot of those doors are optional. We do not have to walk through. We can go around the racism of our childhood, or the sexism. We can make different choices about education, about work, about relationships. It is the great fallacy of the family that the progression is known, that the options are limited, but we, as transfolk, do not get caught up in that. We learn early that there is no one right way. That people who try to defend their One Right Way are scared. We learn that scared people can get mean, quickly, and we also learn how not to be afraid of new pathways, even when no one is holding the door open. And the door is heavy. We have to push hard against it or find the secret knock or the hidden latch. Transfolk will open the door to who we are even when it's difficult, because we do know who we think we are, and this is our strength.

Most of us want to be that person well: most of us want to be good people. Most of us want to perform a gender, a sexuality, that is kind and loving. Most of us think about how we speak to children and elders, people of other genders. We find our way to courtesy and kindness. We find our way to respectful disagreement. And we already know how hard it is to be told that the thing we want or need most is wrong and bad; we know better than to tell that to others (or we should, by gum).

We have thought not only about how much we want to be daughters instead of sons, but why, and what that will mean. We've enjoyed our fantasies and then we have grappled with our realities, and at every turn there has been a cost/benefit analysis. At every turn, we have thought about what it was worth to be who we thought we were.

And how powerful is that? However difficult it also is, we know who we think we are, and we have lived into it. We have decided who we think we are and refashioned ourselves. Let's just say that transfolk, as a community, are not the ones to find ourselves easily thwarted by a difficult task.

And by the way, since we're talking about it, this is a job skill. I think we approach job interviews full of dread, full of fear, hoping that someone will "see past" our trans histories or our trans identities and hire us anyway. The hell with that. "Listen," you should say to your prospective employer. "Listen, now. I was born Louise, in Missouri, in 1971. Between then and now I undertook a substantial process of internal review, identified all the steps required to achieve my goal, including research and investigation of local, state, and federal laws and statutes. I created a budget, managed a financial plan, engaged in medical research and literature review, created a support network for myself, undertook a rigorous program of education and training, negotiated substantial reworking of existing agreements with all constituent parties, and completed all portions of the plan on schedule. My name is now Phil, and you should hire me—if not because I did all that, then because when am I ever going to say to you that something can't be done? When am I ever going to tell you that a task is too complicated?"

We have already learned how not to invest ourselves in someone else's No. We have already heard No a million times in our lives, and we've heard it from the most powerful people in our lives—parents, teachers, religious leaders, medical professionals—and yet we have not been deterred. Maybe for a minute, maybe we have retreated and regrouped and returned again, but we have not let other people's No's run our lives, and we have not let them overrule the Yesses in our hearts. And that is why it is *great* to be trans.

That is, of course, leaving aside the reality of how good it is, how satisfying, to occupy a body you had a hand in creating. Let's think about this. Most people just spend a lot of time complaining about their love handles or dyeing their hair a darker red. And while that's fine—and hey, I'm not that excited about my love handles some days either—it is not the same as taking a good long look at what you're working with and making substantive changes. I know a fabulous transwoman who was once vigorously scolded by a religious fanatic about mutilating the temple of her body. She retorted: I didn't mutilate it. I remodeled the kitchen, I added a breakfast nook, and I put on a little front porch.

Listen, no one is saying you should have surgery, or that you should take hormones, or that there's anything better or worse about any of those options. Well, not true—people are. Other people have all sorts of opinions about what transpeople should or should not do to or with our bodies. I am here to say you can freely ignore them. But I am also here to say that that is, in itself, a miraculous thing. Transpeople have a lot of choices about how we embody ourselves, and I don't just mean physically. We are none of us doing it exactly the way they did it at home. Okay, some things: I am making my grandmother's chicken soup the exact same way she makes it, and I'm not giving that up. But over-all, we have already learned that there is more than one right way. We have already learned that we can remain true to our hearts' desires. That we should.

And some of us are making changes to our bodies. We're tak-ing hormones, we're having surgeries, we're at the gym, we're in the bathroom with a secret tube of mascara brushing it onto our lashes or trying to make our goatees look a little thicker . . . um, maybe that's just me. But regardless, we have our ways. We are making our ways, and we're looking in the mirror every morning for signs of change, and when they happen we are so excited! So pleased to be moving toward what we need to look like, how we need to walk through the world, what it is we need to see when we examine our reflections in the mirror for ourselves. We've taken change in hand, and we've made it, and that is so satisfying. It is like living in a house you built yourself, paddling down the river in a canoe you built with your best friend, making something with great tenderness and great care that will serve you forever and give you a lot of pleasure. And that is why it is *great* to be trans.

While we're talking about pleasure, can I just say this? Queers and transfolk have great sex. We do. No one wants to talk about this. There is a movement afoot in North America that says sex is frivolous and selfish, that if we talk about sex we will not be taken seriously, and so we edit it out. We have learned that when we talk about sex, it makes the religious fundamentalists go bat shit crazy and start lighting up the phone lines, and so we have stopped. We censor ourselves. And that is not fair. Sex is great! It's fun, it feels good, it's good for us—and let me tell you the truth about this. The fundamentalist right wing is not going to like us any better if we don't talk about sex. They will not. They already think we're irredeemably perverted freakshows, so let 'em. I am not going to pretend I don't care about sexual pleasure in order to appease a group of people who are never, ever going to be happy with me anyway. Are you really prepared to let a group of mean strangers guide your life? Guide it more than your own pleasure? Your own wellness?

Queers and trannies, as a group, have better sex. I am sure of this, even though I can't prove it. I can prove that people who have sex an average of once per week over the course of their life-times live longer and report much higher satisfaction with their lives, or at least I can point to the research that says so, and I want us all to live longer. As an elder, I want my world to be populated with old queers and trannies sitting around on the porch telling activist stories and raising up young people into our culture and dropping our napkins repeatedly so that the hunky nursing assistants have to bend down and get them. Ahem. So I'm just going to say this like it's a fact—we are having better sex. We are having amazing, transformative, delicious sex. We started learning about our genders, many of us, through sex, and we learned that we can be anything we want while we're fucking. That's a lot of power, right there; a lot of possibility. While we're busy doing things our own way, nowhere does that exist more than in bed (or alleyway or backseat or over the arm of the couch or whatever you've got going on). We already know that we can try on, or try out, new ways of relating, new genders, new sensibilities. We have already learned to communicate about sex, to say please touch me here and not there, please call my parts this or that, please touch me in a way that makes me feel okay about myself. We've already learned that we can choose not to have sex with people who won't sign on to our comfort as a high priority, and we've learned that if you break the barrier and talk about how you want to be touched, you get to have much better sex.

Much better sex. I am just sayin'.

And we know how to try things out—do we not?—how to evaluate them to see if they are working. And again, we are not so excited as all that about How Everyone Says You're Supposed to Do It, which is a key point for great, hot, intimate, transformative fucking. We do what feels good. We do what makes us shiver. We are not measuring ourselves against porno robots, and we are not letting ourselves get bullied into the idea that there's only one acceptable way to have sex (which often suspiciously matches what the bully in question wants to do). Not that this has never happened to any of us, but we know better now. We know how to say no, thank you, to that. We know how to hold ourselves and others to the higher standard of what actually works for us, in our bodies, right now. And if you're not there yet, honey, come on in—the water's fine. It is okay to want to have sex, it is okay to want to have great sex, and it is okay to want to have playful sex, perverted sex, solo sex, partnered sex, group sex, tender sex, rough sex—all of it. And if all the hot tranny sex isn't a good enough reason to say it's *great* to be trans, then the fact that a university has paid me to come here today and remind you about it is.

We do know how to talk about things, and we know how to share information. We, as a trans community, take on the task of teaching our youngsters and caring for them, whether or not they are chronologically younger than us. We step up to that plate. We are aware that we are needed, that our experience is valuable, that there are people in the world who are tentatively standing in front of the exact same hurdles that we have already cleared, nervously looking at the same flaming hoops we have jumped through, and here is where we are amazing as a community. We do provide advice about hurdle clearing and hoop jumping and fire safety. We say, step here and push off this way. Wear long sleeves. We loan each other money for better metaphorical running shoes. We have even knocked down some of those hurdles for the next people who come along after us. We have extinguished some of those flames. We have not just learned how to master the system, we have started to dismantle it. We are educating doctors and agitating about the Harry Benjamin Standards and establishing WPATH to do better. We are passing along our therapists' names after they have already been pretrained about trans stuff and queer stuff. My therapist likes to joke that I have made him a lot more interesting at cocktail parties. Those of us who are further along, who have more access and privilege and money and power, have used those resources to clear the way for the ones coming up behind us, and you know how rare that is.

You know how much our culture encourages us to consolidate power, to expand privilege, to climb the ladder and then pull it up behind us. But we don't do that. When I was outlining my vision a minute ago about being old trannies together in the old folks' home, raising up our youngsters, everyone nodded along with me. We share a vision that this is vital to the survival of our community, and we are willing to put in some time to mentor the next generation. We are willing to talk about the parts of our experience that are hard for us, even though it would be easier for us to bury them, because we know that information is needed and may help some person we don't even know yet.

We share information, we trade experiences, we field hysterical middle-of-the-night phone calls, we swap doctor referrals. We talk about the great parts. We hand down our clothes and our packers and binders and gaffs and falsies and wigs and spirit gum and who knows what all else. We talk about surgeries, if we've had them, and how they turned out and how much they cost and if we liked our doctors; we show each other our scars, our actual tender places. We make casseroles for the next person having surgery, and we offer to clean their bathrooms for them on week two because only trannies know that the second week after surgery is the moment at which you're finally well enough to be horrified at how grungy your bathroom is but still a little too sore to do much about it. We understand, as a community, that we can take care of each other and we have made a decision, as a community, that we should, even when it's scary. Even when it involves nakedness, or hard conversations, or a toilet brush. And so we do not leave our newest members alone to prove themselves. We help them and we ease their way and we try to get them through the first parts better than we managed when we were there—and that?—that is why it is *great* to be trans.

And while we are evolving, and helping and negotiating and fucking, we are learning like crazy. We are learning how to speak righteously (and not, I am hopeful, self-righteously). But when we are shoved out of our comfort zone, when we recognize that we were born into an enemy camp, we learn how to talk. How to talk about ourselves, how to talk to others, how to explain, how to debate. How to ask questions that lead people to the answers we want them to come to, how to break it down. And while I am endlessly frustrated with the way society feels like it can ask any transperson or genderqueer person or gender-adjacent person any kind of rude or intimate or insulting or probing question anytime it likes, I am also aware that we are using this to our advantage. People think I am crazy when I say this, but I firmly, absolutely believe that a team of transpeople could negotiate a solution to almost any problem, that there should be crackerjack all-tranny negotiation and mediation squads ready to deploy at a moment's notice (and if you think that I have already figured out a totally cute uniform for this squad, you would be correct). But tell me: who has more experience existing on both sides of a border? Who has more experience reframing conflicting or contradictory pieces of information until they eventually complement each other? Who has more experience in continuing to sit down with those who are screaming and crying until they can get their acts together and talk like grown people? And in the real world, we can do it in a walk—and this is why it's *great* to be trans.

Now, are there bad things? Of course there are. Could I give just as long a speech about them? Of course I could. But what I am here to say today, in addition to speaking about all the ways in which being a tranny is fabulous, sexy, honorable, and a good job skill, is to say that we do not have to be defined by the bad things. We can choose to create and tell another story about being trans, one in which the story does not stop when hardships are overcome. A story that makes our triumphs as powerful as our tragedies, that makes our triumphs more powerful than our tragedies, no matter how much the Nice Liberal Ladies who want us to Tell Our Stories encourage us to lean on the hard parts. We can say: "My happy and successful adult life is at least as important as my miserable childhood." We can say: "The hot sex I get to have now is just as valid as the years of celibacy when I never let anyone touch me because I couldn't bear it. " We can say: "All those years I wore clothes I hated are not as important as how fucking fabulous I look now. " We can speak up and speak out about our wellnesses, our pleasures, our satisfactions, and we can choose not to internalize the message that we are pathetic or deceptive creatures.

We can quit practicing the dramatic monologue all the damn time and instead do a little stand-up, and maybe a musical number. We can have a little fun. We may be starting off in life with an especially odiferous batch of shit-smelling compost, some of us, but please let us stop pruning back the gorgeous flowers and the delicious, nourishing vegetables, and the sweet, sweet fruits that grow in the compost so we can point to the mound of shit more effectively. Put the damn shears down. Those good and sweet things? You did that. That is the fruit of your labor, yours and all of ours. That is the gorgeous ground you have cultivated with your hard work and your tender patience and your skills and abilities. Sit and enjoy what is growing, enjoy how far you've come from the mound of shit. Enjoy the people who helped you mulch and hoe and cultivate when there was not much to look at and everything was dirty and it stunk and they stood by you anyway. Revel in it. Sit in the sunshine of having come as far as you have with one of those flowers in your hatband and feel warmed by it. Send some flowers to the worst bully of your childhood, who may still be suffering in the dirty muck of meanness and shame. And then invite everyone you know and like over to dinner. Invite them over, and cook them some of those gorgeous, delicious vegetables that you raised up with your own gorgeous, capable hands, and sit and talk. Sit down with your shared bounty, and talk about how *great* it is to be trans.

S. Bear Bergman is an author of two books and three award-winning solo stage shows, a storyteller, a gender-jammer, and a good example of what happens when you overeducate a contrarian. Ze is also a longtime activist on behalf of queer and trans youth. Bear lives in Southern Ontario with hir husband j wallace, and works at the points of intersection between and among gender, sexuality, and culture (spending most of hir time keeping people from installing traffic signals there).